ISBN: 978129009570

Published by:
HardPress Publishing
8345 NW 66TH ST #2561
MIAMI FL 33166-2626

Email: info@hardpress.net
Web: http://www.hardpress.net

21 Photo

THE GATE

TO THE

𝕳𝖊𝖇𝖗𝖊𝖜, 𝕬𝖗𝖆𝖇𝖎𝖈, 𝖆𝖓𝖉 𝕾𝖞𝖗𝖎𝖆𝖈,

UNLOCKED BY A NEW AND EASY METHOD OF ACQUIRING

THE

ACCIDENCE.

―――

BY THE AUTHOR OF THE GATE TO THE FRENCH,
ITALIAN, AND SPANISH, UNLOCKED.

―――

LONDON:

WILLIAM GOODHUGH, ENGLISH AND FOREIGN BOOKSELLER,

155, OXFORD STREET,

AND GOODHUGH AND RICHARDSON, 4, BERKELEY SQUARE.

―――

1828.

Printed by W. Davy, 8, Gilbert-street, Oxford-street.

JUST PUBLISHED,

BY THE SAME AUTHOR,

THE

ENGLISH GENTLEMAN'S

LIBRARY MANUAL;

OR A

GUIDE TO THE FORMATION OF A LIBRARY

OF

SELECT LITERATURE;

Accompanied with Original Notices, Biographical and Critical, of
Authors and Books.

PREFACE.

Il est de fait que l'etude de l'Hebreu, comme celles des autres langues Orientales, reprend en beaucoup de lieux une nouvelle vie. La Societé Biblique couvrant le monde entier de ses presses et de ses traducteurs, ranime partout la science des livres saints.

CELLERIER.

THE very favorable reception of my little Gate to the French, Italian, and Spanish Languages, (an edition of five hundred copies having been very speedily exhausted,) has encouraged me to finish the present work adapted to the Hebrew, Arabic, and Syriac. Should the present attempt meet with a similar portion of public favor, it is my intention to follow up the plan, by giving cards printed from stone of the various declinable and indeclinable parts of speech, together with the particles and words in most frequent use; likewise forms for parsing and construing, thus presenting an easy introduction to those languages.

The present learned Bishop of Salisbury has published many useful books of this kind, at a moderate price; but the recent invention of printing from stone, has given an increased facility of producing useful elementary works. If any thing need be urged as motives to the study of these ancient and beautiful languages, I am sure the observations I subjoin from learned and eminent men will stimulate to exertion and application.

With respect to the elegance and excellence of the Hebrew language, as contained in the writings of the Old Testament, Mr. Addison, in his Spectator, No. 405, remarks, "There is a certain coldness and indifference in the phrases of our European languages, when they are compared with the Oriental forms of Speech; and it happens very luckily, that the Hebrew idioms run into the English tongue with a peculiar grace and beauty. Our language has received innumerable elegancies and improvements from that infusion of Hebraisms which are derived to it out of the poetical passages in holy writ: they give force and energy to our expression, warm and animate our language, and convey our thoughts in more ardent and intense phrases, than any that are to be met with in our own tongue. There is something so pathetic in this kind of diction, that it often sets the mind in a flame, and makes our hearts burn within us. How cold and dead doth a prayer appear that is composed in the most elegant and polite forms of speech which are natural to our tongue, when it is not heightened by that solemnity of phrase, which may be drawn from the Sacred Writings! It has been said by some of the ancients, that, if the gods were to talk with men, they would certainly speak in Plato's style; but, I think, we may say, with justice, that when mortals converse with their Creator, they cannot do it in so proper a style as in that of the Holy Scriptures.

"If any one would judge of the beauties of poetry that are to be met with in the Divine Writings, and examine how kindly the Hebrew manners of speech mix and incorporate with the English language; after having perused the Book of Psalms, let him read a literal translation of Horace and Pindar, he will find in these two last, such an absurdity and confusion of style, with such a comparative poverty of imagination, as will make him very sensible of what I have been here advancing."

The ingenious and learned Rev. Anthony Blackwall, in his Introduction to the Sacred Classics, observes, "The Hebrew is an original and essential language, that borrows of none, but lends to all. Some of the sharpest Pagan writers, inveterate enemies to the religion and learning of both Jews and Christians, have allowed the Hebrew tongue to have a noble emphasis, and a close and beautiful brevity. The metaphors in that admirable book are apposite and lively; they illustrate the truths expressed by them, and raise the admiration of the reader. The names of men, animals, &c., are very significant. One word is often a good description, and gives you a satisfactory account of the chief and distinguishing property or quality of the thing or person named.

"It would be no difficult matter for a man of diligence and good taste, to prove that the Hebrew Bible has every beauty and excellence that can be found in all the Greek and Roman authors; and a great many more and stronger than any in the most admired classics.

"One might with pleasure enlarge upon numerous instances of the sublimity and admirable beauties of the Old Testament, which are above imitation, and defy criticism and censure."

The learned Buxtorf has proved, that God himself breathed this language into the first parents of mankind.

And Melancthon says, "I prefer the knowledge of the Hebrew before all the wealth of a kingdom."

Even the great reformer, Martin Luther, says, "Although my knowledge of the Hebrew language is but small, yet I would not exchange it for all the wealth of the world."

Henry Ainsworth, the translator of the Pentateuch and Psalms, observes, "that the literal sense of Moses's Hebrew is the ground of all interpretations."

Dr. Bryan Walton, in his Prolegomena to the Polyglot, says, "How absurd is it, that an ambassador should not understand the commands of his king, but depend upon an interpreter for every word he speaks at a foreign court."

The author of the Linguist observes, that "the Hebrew is the most pure, simple, ancient, and radical language. The Hebrew only is from God, and the mother of all other languages."

And another author tells us, that "the Hebrew Scriptures contain the sum of all we can know in divinity and in natural things."

Pere Lamy, in his Introduction to the Holy Scriptures, says, that "the preachers of the gospel are the more inexcusable in neglecting the Scriptures, because they can no where find so rich and inexhaustible a fund for their purpose as there. All the foundations of true eloquence, extraordinary actions, rich expressions, fine examples, apt comparisons, and striking figures, are found in them in great abundance; and all those ornaments which give strength and dignity to discourse.

The Rev. James Hervey, in his Meditations, observes, that "the Hebrew is so pregnant and rich in sense, that no translation can do it justice.

The Rev. Anselm Bayley, LL.D., in the Preface to his Hebrew and English Bible, says, "It is a shame, if not a crime, for the clergy to be unacquainted with this language."

Likewise the late Rev. Mr. Romaine, on the Song of Solomon, asserts, "Without being acquainted with the Hebrew tongue, no man can be a critic upon the writings of the Old Testament."

The late learned and reverend Dr. John Ryland, of Northampton, observes, that "no man can be reckoned a scholar without the knowledge of the Hebrew language: sound human learning cannot exist without the clear knowledge of it. For what is human learning but a knowledge of books and facts, of characters, times, and ages, the original springs of action, and our connection with God, and all mankind? But how can this be attained, except by a familiar acquaintance with that admirable book, which discovers the natural and moral perfections of God; the origin and structure of the universe, our incessant dependance on the universal agency of God, the ultimate design of our immortal powers, and the last end of the whole creation? In a word, if there be any ambition to excel, in the ingenuous part of the British youth; if there be any love and admiration of vital virtue; if there be any desire to rise above the vulgar and ignorant part of mankind; if you have any clear sense of the noble, the beautiful, and the affecting, you will seize the opportunity of being made acquainted with the sacred literature, now the thorns and briars, the brambles and stinging nettles, are removed from the passage, and the path to the sacred language is strewed with flowers."

Such indeed are the testimonies of many great and learned men, who have all taken a peculiar delight in the study of this most ancient language; and where can it be found in its purity, but in the Oracles of Truth, which were dictated by God himself, and communicated to us by the blessed instruments of his inspiration? In fact, the Hebrew has an emphatic energy, which it is not in the power of any version to equal; and if we could understand the Scriptures without it, yet it would be a sufficient motive to stimulate us to the study of it, because it has been consecrated by the mouth of the Almighty.

The Arabic language is undoubtedly one of the most ancient in the world, and arose soon after, if not at, the confusion of Babel. There were several dialects of it very different from each other: the most remarkable was that spoken by the tribe of Hamyar, and the other genuine Arabs, and that of the Koreish. The Hamyaritic seems to have approached nearer to the purity of the Syriac than the dialect of any other tribe; for the Arabs acknowledge their father Yarab to have been the first whose tongue deviated from the Syriac (which was his mother-tongue, and is almost generally acknowledged by the Asiatics to be the most ancient,) to the Arabic.

The dialect of the Koreish is usually termed the pure Arabic, or as the Korân, which is written in this dialect, calls it the perspicuous and clear Arabic;

perhaps, says Dr. Pocock, because Ismael, their
father, brought the Arabic he had learned of the
Jorhamites nearer to the original Hebrew. But the
politeness and elegance of the Koreish is rather to
be attributed to their having the custody, of the
Caába, and dwelling in Mecca, the centre of Arabia,
as well as more remote from intercourse with foreigners, who might corrupt their language. The Arabic
is harmonious and expressive; and withal so copious, that they say no man without inspiration can
be a perfect master of it in its utmost extent.

I should feel great pleasure in contributing my
aid in the formation of a Language Society, on a
similar plan to that described at the end of this volume; and would cheerfully render my assistance to
those who might be inclined to come forward for
that purpose.

October, 1827.

LANGUAGES.

THE similitude and derivation of languages afford the most indubitable proof of the traduction of nations, and the genealogy of mankind. They often add physical certainty to historical evidence, and supply the only evidence of ancient migrations, and of the revolutions of ages which left no written monuments behind them.

"Every man's opinions, at least his desires, are a little influenced by his favourite studies.' My zeal for languages may seem perhaps rather overheated, even to those by whom I desire to be well esteemed. To those who have nothing in their thoughts but trade or policy, present power, or present money, I should not think it necessary to defend my opinions; but with men of letters I would not unwillingly compound, by wishing the continuance of every language, however narrow in its extent, or however incommodious for common purposes, till it is reposited in some version

B

of a known book, that it may be always hereafter examined and compared with other languages, and then permitting its disuse. For this purpose the translation of the Bible is most to be desired."—Dr. Johnson.

In a work of this kind, some notices of the literature and mode of education, as practised among the Jews, and several of the eastern nations, may not be unacceptable

EDUCATION

Of the Jewish Schools.

The Jewish doctors carry their information on this subject to a very high antiquity, and assert that Cain applied himself to the invention of mechanical arts; his younger brother Seth instructed his posterity in virtuous practices, and was skilled in astronomy; he erected two noble pillars for the preservation of that knowledge which should stand the shock of an universal deluge—Josephus is positive that one of them was extant in his time.

Noah in blessing his son Japhet, says, "that he shall dwell in the tents of Sem." Several expositors understand this of the schools of Sem, which were also famous in the days of Rebecca, as alluded to in the Chaldee Paraphrase. These schools were afterwards supported by Heber, from whom the Hebrews took their name; the Jewish doctors say that Jacob studied in the schools of Sem and Heber. Abraham, they say, raised himself to a wonderful eminence in all branches of knowledge; he came to a knowledge of the only true God by his

contemplation of the heavenly bodies, and the wonderful harmony in the works of creation ; assisted with
the singular blessing of Heaven, he therefore forsook
his idolatrous country and became a zealous promoter
of the worship and service of the true God. It is said
that he removed the souls he had gotten ; the Chaldee
Paraphrase interprets this, of the souls he had subdued to
the law of his God ; and other expositors, of the souls
he had proselyted and converted from Paganism.

When Jacob journeyed to Succoth, and built him
a house—that is, as Philo renders it, a house and tents
to the Lord—in the Chaldee house of learning ; as
also where it is said of Joseph, that he taught Pharoah's
senators wisdom, that is, imparted knowledge to
them.

After the deliverance from the captivity, no considerable number of the Jews settled at any time or
place, without appointing some public teachers and
public schools. In particular places, every congregation was obliged to take the care of furnishing out a
place of public education ; whoever neglected this,
made themselves liable to an Anathema.

God commanded Moses to appoint and choose seventy of the elders, men of wisdom, understanding,
integrity, and all those qualities that enable others to
judge and teach, to assist him in the government and
to instruct the people. He accordingly chose and appointed them, himself being chief, constituting a
senate or consistory of seventy-one, which, by way of
excellence, was called the Great Consistory, and latterly, the Sanhedrim. They were the fountain source
of wisdom and learning to the whole nation, being in-
vested with all manner of jurisdiction. They had

power' to depute and appoint lesser consistories of twenty-three : two of which were in Jerusalem, the one at the door of the court of the temple, and one in every city throughout all Israel, who had likewise power to teach and instruct the people in their respective districts, and to approve of and promote lesser schools ; to judge and answer any questions concerning the true sense and interpretation of scripture, and in points of great difficulty were to apply to the great consistory, which was constantly held at Jerusalem, in the paved chamber near the temple. This constitution first gave rise to their regular schools, and lasted until the destruction of the temple. .

The Prophet Samuel presided in a school called Naioth, or Ramah, where he instructed the people in matters of policy, in which respect he was their judge ; and in matters of religion as their doctor or public teacher. Hence it is that the jewish expositors, by the company of prophets, generally understand the scholars under his charge and tuition, (I Samuel, xix. 18, 19, 20) and by the word *Naioth*, a public school.

The next considerable place of public teaching was the College, or school of Jerusalem, mentioned in Kings, xxii. 14 ; where we are informed that Josiah, upon hearing the book of the law, presented and read to him by Halkiah the priest, and reflecting upon the manifold corruptions of his time, rent his clothes, and sent to inquire of the Lord ; that is, sent some special messengers to Huldah the prophetess, who was then in the school of Jerusalem, and in conferring with whom, they were instructed in the will of the Lord. Afterwards Jehoshaphat, moved by the same consideration, appointed not only schools in the chief

C a

cities but also in all parts of his kingdom, and sent eminent men for teachers, who should everywhere instruct the people in the true worship and service of God. 2 Chron. xvii.

From the time of this good prince, until the Babylonish captivity, schools flourished or decayed, according as they were supported by good, or discountenanced by wicked kings.

The School of the the Prophets, over which Elisha presided, was so numerous, that application was made for enlarging the building, which was represented to him as too small; Elisha complied with the request, and encouraged the work by his personal assistance, even to a miracle. 2 Kings, vi. 1—6.

During the time of the captivity in Babylon, schools were kept up and supported, as the Jews were always allowed the freedom of their own law. Daniel at this time had acquired so great a reputation for wisdom and learning, that he was consulted by Nebuchadnezzar about that remarkable vision, which all the wise men of his kingdom had in vain attempted to make known. His reputation was still more enhanced by the great service he did Belshazzar, in regard to the fearful handwriting on the wall.

When it pleased God to deliver his people out of captivity, the schools began to flourish again. When Cyrus had published his royal edict for the rebuilding of Jerusalem, (foretold by the prophet, Isaiah xliv. 45) we find by the interposition of their adversaries, whose services were not accepted in the building, an interruption for some time took place, by a decree of Artaxerxes, surnamed Longimanus; but Darius, commonly called Nothus, otherwise the Syrian, having rein-

forced the decree of Cyrus, Ezra undertook the pious
work, and by an unwearied diligence brought it to
perfection.

Ezra is thought by some to be the same with Malachi,
the prophet. In Malachi, i. 1. it is said, "the burthen
of the word of the Lord to Israel, by the hand of Malachi." The Chaldee Paraphrase adds, who is called
Ezra the scribe. His accomplishments were very
extraordinary ; he is said to have been a ready scribe
in the law of Moses, and was a person of very great
abilities, which qualified him to digest the Holy Scriptures into the order and method in which they now
appear.—He added the points, which are used to this
day. And of no less integrity, for he "prepared his
heart to seek the law of his God, and to do it, and to
teach in Israel statutes and judgements," Ezra, vii. In
his time was instituted the great synagogue of the
hundred and twenty elders, whereof he was a principal
member, and which continued until the days of Simeon,
surnamed the just, who was one of this number, and
the same who received Alexander the great, upon his
approach to Jerusalem, in the course of his victories.
In succeeding ages many celebrated schools were
maintained, particularly those of Javne, Tiberias,
Sipora, and many more which were situated in Judæa ;
over these schools presided many celebrated and
learned doctors. In this rank may justly be placed
those two eminent men, Hillel and Shammai.
Learning thus continued to flourish in Judæa, and
was promoted and cultivated until the days of Judas,
surnamed the Holy, who was author of the Mishna.
After his decease, two of his principal scholars, de-
parting from Judæa into Babylon, erected schools, and

drew after them the greatest part of the doctors; though it is not probable that even then Palestine was destitute of learning, nor that the schools were quite shut up. The Talmudists expressly assert the contrary.

The principal schools in Babylon were those of Nahardea, Sora, and Pumbeditha; they flourished in Babylon until the year of the world, 4797, as appears from the names of the chief rulers and doctors residing there, preserved in the Chronicles of the Jews.

At this era, the Jews being dispersed all over the world, these schools ceased, but wherever a competent number met and settled into a community, their first care was to erect schools; many of them had great renown in various countries of Europe, as Spain, Portugal, Germany, and likewise in the Persian and Turkish dominions. Funds were provided and settled, according to the greater or lesser number of those to be instructed, and in case of refusal, the greater cities had power to excommunicate. Every master of a family was obliged to maintain a tutor at his own private charge, until his children be out of the lower forms, and had, by their proficiency in learning, qualified themselves for the higher schools.

Two of the chief men in every synagogue were appointed yearly, about the day of Pentecost, whose duty it was to take care of the schools; they were likewise to take care that the youth in the synagogue perform their devotions solemnly and regularly, with power to inflict punishment.

The qualifications of masters of schools were, that they should possess considerable intellectual abilities, and of known probity and integrity; their lives comporting with their doctrine, that they might be able to instruct both by precept and example. The scholars were expected to be of a humble and docile disposition, that they should behave themselves with modesty, and an agreeable reverence to their teachers; in every way to be qualified by virtue and good manners to reap the benefits of their instruction. Should either master or scholar be found incapable of rising to a sufficient pitch of learning, he was to be removed and sent to some meaner employment, it being thought inconsistent with the honour and dignity of the law to be handled by persons of inferior abilities. No child was to be admitted in the public schools under six years of age, they were then to be prepared by being accustomed to repeat some principal texts of the law, as " Hear, O Israel, the Lord our God is one Lord," &c. Upon their first admission, they were to be instructed in the law of Moses, the text and historical passages, with the writings of the prophets, it being considered most proper that their first advances in learning should have their foundation in religion, that both might grow up together. After this, they were to proceed to the Oral Law, or Mishna, whereby they are to be instructed in the literal sense and meaning of the written law, being already acquainted with the text. The masters were accustomed to propound allegories and parables to their scholars, under which some useful piece of knowledge was concealed, and required them to find out the allusion.

On reference to history, this practice will be found to have very generally obtained among philosophers and poets in the East.

From this they advanced to logic, then to natural

philosophy, and some part of mathematical science; and lastly, to metaphysics.

Natural philosophy was taught from the first chapter of the book of Genesis, and was called the study of the work of creation.

Their metaphysics were grounded upon the first chapter of Ezekiel.

The number of scholars allowed to the care of one master was twenty-five, should the number increase to forty, the master was obliged to take an assistant.

In the greater schools, the number was not precisely determinable, amounting sometimes to three or four hundred, according to the populousness of the place; in these, the masters read in the quality of professors.

The scholars were obliged to pay the same honour to their masters as to their parents, upon which account they were not permitted to call them by their own names, but that of master. No person was permitted to become a teacher, unless he had conferred upon him the necessary degrees required to fit him for that charge. This was done before the congregation by laying on of hands, and he was then taken by the hand and placed in a chair, appointed for that purpose. In some places, a book of the law was put into his hand, and he was proclaimed a teacher or doctor. The title was different in various places, though the most general was that of Rabbi. The practice had its origin in ancient times, as in Deut. xxxiv. 9, "And Joshua, the son of Nun, was full of the spirit of wisdom, for Moses had laid his hands upon him."

Literature, and Learned Men of the Jews.

THE MISHNA.

This great work, which is most ancient and venerable, contains an account of all those doctrines and practices which were delivered by Moses himself, and continued and preserved to posterity, by oral tradition, until the foundation of the second temple.   B.C. 347.

In this period, the great synagogue flourished, being supported by some of the prophets, and other persons of eminence, such as Haggai, Malachi, Mordecai, Ezra, &c. the last of this great synagogue was Simeon, surnamed the just; he was president of the great school, and he was the same, who is called in the Mishna Iddo, or Jaddus, the high priest.

In the next period, Antigonus Sochotensis was president, B.C. 308, whose scholar was Sadoc, who, by perverting and abusing his master's doctrine, gave birth to the opinions of the Sadducees, touching the resurrection and rewards in a future state.   Antigonus taught that we were obliged to serve God out of pure love, and not out of a prospect of being rewarded by him, from which Sadoc inferred, that there shall be no rewards in another life, nor, consequently, any resurrection from the dead.

In the fourth period, which occurs B.C. 260, there was Jose Ben Joezer, and Jose Ben Johanan; as also R. Eleazar, the high priest, who sent seventy-two elders to Ptolemy, to be employed in the translation of the Bible, usually called the septuagint version.

To these succeeded, in the next period, B.C. 251;
Joshua the son of Perechias—Johanan, the son of
Matthias, the high priest; and Nittai, the Arbelite.

After these flourished, B.C. 134, Judah the son of
Tabbai, and Simeon the son of Sattah.

In the seventh period, B.C. 38, the rulers were
Shemaiah and Abtaleon, who were not jews originally
but proselytes, and were descended from King Senna-
cherib, as is reported by tradition.

The next period was B.C. 32, in which the two
eminent doctors Hillel and Shammai flourished; as
also the celebrated Jonathan Ben Uziel, the author of
the Chaldee Paraphrase upon the Pentateuch, and
some other parts of the bible; together with R. Nehem-
nias the son of Kannah, who wrote a profound and
elaborate discourse on the Cabbala, or Scripture Myste-
ries, entitled Sepher-Habbahir, of which only some
parts are in print. He wrote, likewise, another book
concerning the Tetragrammaton. There were likewise,
at this time, R. Hannania Ben Hezekia, who composed a book entitled Megillath Tannith, which gives
an historical relation of the afflictions and troubles
that have happened to the jewish nation, and the
miraculous deliverances which were vouchsafed to
them, from whence fasts or feasts were instituted.
In the Talmud, this work is inserted next to the
Mishna.

The ninth period occurs in the year of our Lord 8;
at which time, Rabban Simeon Ben Hillel the elder
flourished; he was the first to whom the title of Rabban
was attributed, which afterwards continued to the
chief ruler of the Sanhedrim; before they were only
called by their proper names. There was also R.

Johanan Ben Zacchee, who lived above one hundred and twenty years, and-bred up a great many eminent and learned men.

The next period, A.D. 28, is remarkable for the removal of the great Sanhedrim from the temple of Jerusalem to the school of Jabne, where learning was attended with those advantages and encouragements, which, during the troubles at Jerusalem, could not be expected; and here R. Simeon the second, the son of Gamaliel, began to preside, A.D. 50, being eighteen years before the destruction of the temple. He was a few years afterwards one of the ten most eminent martyrs who suffered for their constant adherence to their religion.

The above relation mentions a few of the eminent men noticed in the Mishna until the destruction of the temple, from which a new era begins, and includes a notice of some celebrated in their respective periods until the Mishna was committed to writing. In the first period, A.D. 73, after the martyrdom of R. Simeon; R. Johanan Ben Zacchee, retiring to Jabne, was constituted ruler of the Sanhedrim, in which honourable post he continued until his death. At this time, likewise, flourished R. Gamaliel the second; as also R. Eliezer the great, the son of Hircanus, who composed several treatises, particularly one entitled Orchoth Charim, being a moral discourse, designed to promote the government and regulation of men's lives, according to the rules of virtue; which was printed at Constantinople, Venice, and Cracow; and another entitled *Perke Eliezer*, wherein he comprises the history of the world, deducing it down to the time of R. Gamaliel the second. This book was printed at

Venice in 1544; there is another book under this name, quoted by the title of Tzavaath R. Eliezer, being of the same argument with the first, and directed to his son by way of legacy.

In the second period, which is in the year of Christ 80, flourished R. Akibah, and presided over the Sanhedrim. He was a proselyte, and was supposed to have been of the posterity of Sisera. The following treatises are assigned to him:—Othioth, wherein he expounds, alphabetically, the Cabbala, printed at Cracow. Jetzirah, or Sepher Jetzirah, that is, the book of creation, a celebrated cabbalistical treatise printed in the year 1560. Mechilta, a mystical commentary, or an allegorical exposition of some sections of the book of Exodus, printed at Venice 1520.

There are other books upon this subject, which, though not written by him, are yet all of them composed agreeably to his doctrine; as Siphra, Siphri, &c. In this period, Onkelos flourished, celebrated for his Chaldee paraphrase upon the Bible; as also R. Ishmael, and R. Ishmael Ben Elisha, who published several books, particularly a cabbalistical treatise, entitled Enoch, or Pirke Hechaloth, quoted in the Zohar, printed at Venice; and a discourse, called the Thirteen Ways of expounding the Law, which is annexed to the Siphra before mentioned.

In the third period, A.D. 121, flourished R. Simeon the third, the son of R. Gamaliel the second; and R. Meyr, who was a proselyte, and others. At this time, also, lived R. Simeon Ben Jochai, author of the Zohar, an abstruse cabbalistical commentary upon the Pentateuch; it was printed at Cremona in 1559, and at Mantua in 1558. Throughout the Talmud, honourable mention is made of this rabbi, not only for his great attainments in cabbalistical learning, but also for his extraordinary abilities and skill in deciding many grave questions in the law. There is a book, called Siphri, which likewise goes under his name—a mystical and allegorical exposition of the books of Numbers and Deuteronomy. Contemporary to these, was also R. Joseph Ben Halaphta, who published a chronological treatise, called Seder Olam Rabba, from the creation of the world, to the time of the Emperor Hadrian. He was the master of R. Judas, surnamed the holy; there was also R. Nathan the Babylonian, who wrote a treatise, entitled Pirke avoth, containing an account of the moral apothegms, and pious sentences of the fathers of the jewish church. This book is inserted in the body of the Talmud.

The fourth and last period of the authors of the Mishna, was A.D. 153, in which flourished R. Juda, commonly styled Rabbenu Hokkadosh, that is, our holy doctor, who committed to writing all the doctrines and practices of the jewish church, which had been conveyed down to his time by oral tradition. The great work of the Mishna was completed A.D. 218.

An Account of the Books of the Mishna.

The First is entitled Zerahim, and treats of all those laws, which concern seeds, fruits, herbs, &c. with their uses; this part comprises eleven books—

The 1st of which is called *Berachoth*, that is *Blessings*, containing prayers and thanksgivings for the fruits of the earth.

The 2d is called *Peah*, that is a corner; treating of the obligation to leave some parts or corners of the ground for the benefit of the poor, to be gleaned by them.

The 3d is called *Demai*, that is a doubtful thing; treats of those things concerning which there is a doubt whether or not tithes have been paid of them.

The 4th is called *Kilaim*, that is heterogeneous things; on the unlawfulness of mixing, or joining together, things of a different nature or kind.

The 5th is called *Sheviith*, that is the seventh; on the laws of the sabbatical year—land was to rest and lie fallow, debts were to be remitted and so on.

The 6th is called *Teroumoth*, that is oblations; on the things each man was compelled to set apart and offer as holy to the Priest.

The 7th is called *Maaseroth*, that is the tenths; treating on the law of tithes.

The 8th is called *Maaser Sheni*, that is the second tenths; on the laws of the second tithes, which the Levites received.

The 9th is called *Challa*, that is a cake; treating on the law which compelled the Israelites to set apart a cake of their dough for the priests.

The 10th is called *Orlah*, that is circumcision.

The 11th is called *Biccurim*, that is first fruits; on what things, and after what manner first fruits were to be offered in the temple.

The Second general head is called *Moed*, and treats of all those laws which were given concerning festivals and days of solemn observation;

The 1st is an account of the Sabbath Day, and all the solemnities proper to be observed therein.

The 2d is called *Eruvim,* that is associations; shewing how the food gathered, and put together by several neighbours, should unite them in concord as if belonging to one family.

The 3d is called *Posachim* ; treating of all the rites of the passover.

The 4th is called *Shekalim* ; on the shekels to be paid every year, towards the daily sacrifice.

The 5th is called *Joma,* which treats of the great day of expiation, and the solemnities to be observed on the occasion.

The 6th is called *Sukka* ; giving an account of the feast of Tabernacles.

The 7th is called *Batza* called likewise *Jom Tofe* ; which shews what things may or may not be lawfully undertaken on any festival, except the sabbath.

The 8th is called *Rish Hoshanna* ; giving an account of the laws and solemnities of the feast of the new year.

The 9th is called *Taanith* ; treating of the various fasts and rites throughout the year.

The 10th is called *Megilla* ; treating on the feast of Purim, and gives directions how the Book of Esther should be read.

The 11th is called *Moedkaton* ; which shews what works may lawfully be done on the second, third, fourth, fifth, and sixth days, when the first and seventh are holy—these intermediate days being lesser festivals.

The 12th is called *Chagiga* ; giving an account how persons ought to be qualified to appear before the Lord at the three great solemnities of the year.

The Third general head, entitled *Nashin*, treats of the laws pertaining to women, as marriages, divorces, &c. and are comprised in the following books.

The 1st is called *Jehammoth*; on the law obliging the brother to marry his brother's widow, and what ceremonies were to accompany it.

The 2d is called *Kethubboth*; discoursing on the law of dowries.

The 3d is called *Kiddushin*; treating on the laws of betrothing.

The 4th is called *Gittin*; on the laws of divorcement.

The 5th is called *Nedarim*; giving an account of what vows are obligatory.

The 6th is called *Nasir*; on the laws relating to the Nazarites.

The 7th is called *Sota*; on the laws touching an adulterous woman.

The Fourth general head, called *Nezichin*, treats of the injuries done either by man or beast, what punishment may legally be inflicted on the party offending, and what reparation to the party offended; comprising the following books.

The 1st is called *Bava-Kama*; on the damages sustained from either man or beast.

The 2d is called *Bava-Metzia*; on the laws of usury —letting to hire.

The 3d is called *Bava-Bathra*; on the laws relating to commerce, buying and selling—the laws of inheritances.

The 4th is called *Sanhedrim*; giving an account of the great senate, and other inferior courts of judicature.

The 5th is called *Makkoth*; treating of the forty

C

;stripes, and the reason, the Rabbies subtracted one from the number.

The 6th is called *Shevrioth*; treating on the law of oaths.

The 7th, on the nature of evidence and decisions of important questions, collected from the testimonies of some of the most celebrated Rabbies.

The 8th is called *Horaioth*; on the punishment of persons acting in opposition to the decrees of the Sanhedrim.

The 9th is called *Avoda Zara*, or *Avodath Chochabim*; treating on idolatory.

The 10th is called *Aboth*; giving an historical account of those fathers, who, in their respective ages, delivered the oral law; with the moral sayings and maxims of the fathers.

The Fifth general head, called *Kodashim*, treats of the laws relative to sacrifices, and all religious performances; containing eleven books.

The 1st is called *Zebachim*; treating on the nature of sacrifices.

The 2d is called *Cholin*; treating of the clean and unclean animals.

The 3d is called *Menachoth*; treating of the oblations of flour, oil, and wine, proper to each sacrifice.

The 4th is called *Bechoroth*; treating of the first-born of living creatures, and how they are to be offered or redeemed with money.

The 5th treats of the valuation and tithing of such things as are devoted to the service of the Almighty, in order to their being redeemed.

The 6th is called *Temurah*; shewing how far it may be allowed to exchange one sacred thing for another.

The 7th is called *Meilah*; explaining the nature of sacrilege.

The 8th is called *Kerittoth*; explaining the nature of the punishment of the law—which is called, " being cut off from his people."

The 9th is called *Tamid*; treating of the daily sacrifice, and when it was to be offered.

The 10th is called *Middoth*; discoursing of the dimensions and proportions of the temple.

The 11th is called *Kinnim*; treating of the turtles, or young pigeons, the poor were obliged to offer.

The Sixth general head, called *Taharoth*, treats of the general laws relating to pollutions and purifications.

The 1st is called *Kelim*; treating of the pollutions incident to vessels, &c.

The 2d is called *Oholoth*; shewing how such pollutions are contracted.

The 3d is called *Negahim*; discoursing on the laws relating to leprosy.

The 4th is called *Parah*; shewing how uncleanness, contracted by approaching a dead body, may be purified by the ashes of a red heifer.

The 5th is called *Taharoth*; treating of other kinds of pollutions.

The 6th is called *Mikvaoth*; on the laws relating to baths appointed for purification.

The 7th is called *Nidda*; on the laws relating to the pollutions and purifications of women.

The 8th is called *Machsirin*; on the pollution received by seeds or fruits in the mixture of liquids.

The 9th is called *Zabim*; on purification of persons afflicted.

The 10th *Tibbul Jom*; on uncleanness, however contracted, that is not done away until the going down of the sun.

The 11th is called *Judaiim*; on the ceremonies observed in washing the hands.

The 12th is called *Oketzim*; on the touching of the stalk, how any sort of fruit may derive a pollution.

This comprises the whole body of the Mishna.

When the Mishna was committed to writing, it was received as an authentic body of the law, and taught in all their public schools.

The Mishna being composed of aphorisms, and short sentences, it was considered requisite to give explanations, to render it more easy and intelligible; this is what is called—

The Gemara,

and the authors of it, Æmoræi, or Gemarists. It was first commenced at Jerusalem, in the time of R. Judas: his two sons were the first expositors. R. Oshaya Rabba, also, wrote a treatise called Bereshith Rabba, or an exposition of the Mishna, and another called Tosaphtha. R. Johanan, in the year of the world 3990, composed the Talmud of Jerusalem, which Talmud is very brief, and does not reach the whole of the Mishna, because it was composed for the use of the schools in the Holy Land; it has been printed at Venice, by Bomberg; and at Cracow, with references.

The most celebrated of their schools were those of Pumbeditha, Nahardea, and Sora.

R. Abina, who was rector of the school of Sora, completed the Talmud of Babylon, A. D. 500.

- The Talmud comprises both the Mishna and

Gemara: every Mishna goes before, by way of text; the Gemara is subjoined as a comment; making a comprehensive body of all the jewish learning.

The great author of the Mishna, R. Ashe, propounds four things to be insisted on.

First.—The declaring the reasons, and explaining the grounds upon which every Mishna is established.

Second.—The deciding of points controverted amongst the doctors, and directing whom to follow in practice.

Third.—The decrees and ordinances enacted from the days of R. Juda to his own time.

Fourth.—Some mystical expositions of the law, and parabolical histories, not to be understood according to the letter, but in a figurative sense, and with design to instruct in useful precepts of morality, as has always been the practice of the oriental nations.

PART II.

VERSIONS OF THE NEW TESTAMENT.

Syriac Version.

The Syriac version is generally acknowledged to be very ancient; according to the Syrian Christians, part of the Old Testament was translated in the time of Solomon. As there were in the earliest ages of Christianity, some christians beyond the Euphrates, most of whom, as not being subject to the Roman Empire, understood neither Greek nor Latin, M. Simon supposes that they soon got a version of the New Testament.

Armenian Version,

Is said by the historians of that nation, to have been done in the beginning of the fifth century.

Coptic Version.

Some authors consider it was done in the fourth or fifth century; it agrees in many particulars with the Armenian—it was made from the Greek.

Ethiopic Version.

The Ethiopic version was the first of all those made in the eastern languages, that ever was printed; some suppose it was done in the third century.

Ancient versions serve to clear many passages, because most of them were made, if not from the originals, at least from more ancient copies than any we now have; the earliest is called the Italic version, because it was made in Italy, for the use of the Latins. It was used till the sixth century. There are some parts of it to be seen in the margins of some ancient manuscripts. Dr. Mill supposes it was done in the second century. To this succeeds the Vulgate, or the version of St. Jerome; towards the end of the fourth century, he undertook to revise the Italic, and render it more conformable to the Greek.

Origin of the Chaldee Paraphrases.

After the Hebrew language ceased to be the mother tongue of the Jews, the Holy Scriptures, were from that time forward, interpreted in their synagogues, either in Greek or Chaldee, which afterwards gave rise to the Chaldee Paraphrases now extant; such are those of Onkelos, and Jonathan. Some are of opinion this custom was established by Ezra, it was performed in the following manner :—the minister (or any other person appointed to read) read one verse in the original Hebrew, then stopped to let the interpreter speak, who, standing near him, rendered the whole into the vulgar tongue.

The Cabbala,

Or the doctrine received by tradition—it consisted of two parts, one of which contains the opinions, rites, and ceremonies of the Jews, the other the mystical expositions of the law—which they called the oral law. This Cabbala was of a very ancient date, and was the occasion of most of the heresies among Christians. The Jews had a great regard for these traditions, looking upon them as the key of the law.

Omission of Daniel among the Prophets, by the Jews.

Maimonides assigns as a reason for the omission, that every thing that Daniel wrote, was not revealed to him when awake, and had the use of his reason ; but in the night only, and in obscure dreams.

The Sephiroth.

The Sephiroth of the Cabbala, were certain number-ings which were used, to signify the attributes of God, as creator and governor of the world; the names of these Sephiroth, were crown, wisdom, under-standing, magnificence, severity, glory, victory, foundation and kingdom.

The Synagogue of the Jews.

Synagogues are so frequently mentioned in the New Testament, that it is necessary we should have a correct notion of them ; they were considered holy places ; the Greek word, as well as the Hebrew, to which it answers, signifies any assembly, whether holy, or profane. The Christians often gave the name of synagogues to their assemblies.

They were first used by the Jews after the Babylonish captivity ; they were erected, not only in towns, and cities, but also in the country, near rivers, that they might always have water ready at hand. They were not allowed to build one in any town, unless there were ten persons of leisure in it or persons of learning and approved integrity, free from all worldly occupations, and disengaged from civil affairs. After a synagogue was built, it was consecrated by prayer.

Belonging to the synagogues were :—

First.—The ark, or chest, which contained the book of the law, or Pentateuch—the writings of the prophets were not laid therein. Before it, there was a vail, representing the vail which separated the holy place from the holy of holies.

Second.—The pulpit, with a desk in the middle of the synagogue, in which he who was to expound the law stood up.

Third.—The seats, or pews, wherein the people sat to hear the law read and expounded, some of which were more honorable than others, which were for the elders. These elders sat with their backs towards the ark, and their faces to the congregation, who looked towards the ark.

These seats are called in the gospels, the *chief seats*, which our Saviour ordered his disciples not to contend for, as the Pharisees did.

Rules of the Synagogue.

To regulate, and take care of all things belonging to the synagogue service, there was appointed a council, or assembly of grave and wise persons, well versed in the law, over whom was set a president, who was called ruler of the synagogue.

Their Office.

It was the office of the rulers of the synagogue, to teach the people; this they did sometimes by way of dispute and conference; by questions and answers; or by continued discourses, like sermons. All these different ways of teaching, they called by the general name of searching: the discourse, they styled a search, or inquisition; and him that made it, a searcher, from a Hebrew word, which signifies to dive into the sublime, profound, mystical, allegorical and prophetical senses of Holy Scripture. St. Paul asks the Corinthians, "where is the profound searcher of this world?" it is evident, from the epistle to the Hebrews, that the apostle sometimes followed this mystical method.

The Upper Room, or House-top.

There were several places, set apart for these searches, or expositions ; sometimes in private houses, for there was no Jew of any learning, but what had, in the upper part of his house, one or more rooms, where he was wont, at certain times, to retire, either to pray, or to meditate upon the law ; several instances of persons retiring on the *house-top*, to exercise them-selves in works of piety and devotion, are to be met with in the sacred writings ; they were called by the Latins *Cœnacula*. It was in one of these our Saviour celebrated his last passover ; and in a like place, where the apostles assembled together, when the Holy Ghost came down upon them.

Preaching of Christ in the Synagogue.

"It may seem strange, that the Jews should suffer Jesus Christ, or his disciples, to preach in their syna-gogues, but our wonder will cease, if we consider, first, that they were Jews, and strict observers of the law ;—secondly, that they were well versed in the law, and even were Rabbins, or Doctors—that Jesus Christ was so, is unquestionably certain, since he is fre-quently called Rabbi by his disciples, and even by the Jews themselves."

It is evident, from the New Testament and eccle-siastical history, that the sermons and discourses, spoken by the primitive Christians, were regulated much after the same manner, as those that were delivered in the ancient synagogue of the Jews.

Ministers of the Synagogue.

In the synagogue, there were several ministers, who had different employments assigned them ;—First, one called *Sheliach Zibbor*, or the messenger, or angel of the synagogue, standing before the ark, repeated the prayer *Kadesh*, before and after the reading of the law. Hence it is, that the bishops of the seven churches of Asia, are called the angels of those churches, because, what the Sheliach Zibbor did in the synagogue, that did the bishop in the church. Second, another was called the minister of the synagogue, who from the pulpit, gave the Levites notice when they were to sound the trumpet ; this minister, sometimes read the law. The third, was called *Chaan*, that is, the guardian or keeper ; his business was to take the book of the law out of the ark, and give it to the person appointed to read, and to take it of him, after he had done, and to lay it up in the chest again ; he blew the trumpet upon some particular occasions, to give notice of the sabbath ; of the new year ; to publish an excommunication ; to let the people know when they should say Amen, and to take care of the synagogue.

Synagogue Service.

The synagogue service was three times a day, morning, afternoon, and evening ; Mondays, Thursdays and Saturdays, were considered more solemn than the rest. On the Sabbath-day they had prayers four times. Before the public prayers, the people repeated several private ones, they were nineteen in number: the first, contained praises to God;—second, the confession of their sins;—third, thanksgivings and petitions for all the wants and necessities of this life, as well spiritual as temporal; when these prayers were ended, the minister standing up, began the public prayers, the people likewise standing. They had also their heads covered with a vail.

Their service began and ended with the prayer Kadesh, it was composed in these terms:—

"Hallowed be his great Name in the World which he has created according to his good pleasure, and may his kingdom be established; may we behold his redemption spring up and flourish; may his Messiah suddenly appear in our days, and in the days of all the house of Israel to deliver his people."

Prayers being ended, the minister took out the book of the law, which consisted of several rolls of vellum, stitched or placed together, and fastened to sticks, neatly turned.

The Jews divided the Pentateuch into sections, which they called Paraschahs, one of which being read every Sabbath-day, the whole Pentateuch was thus read over once a year; after the reading of the *law*, followed that of the prophets, before which they rehearsed some passage out of the writings of Moses.

The Law and the Prophets.

By the law and the prophets mentioned in the New Testament, we are to understand, the five books of Moses, and the Prophets, the books of Joshua, Judges, Samuel, Kings, and Chronicles, these they supposed to have been written by prophets, which they called former prophets; they next placed Isaiah, Jeremiah and Ezekiel, with the twelve lesser prophets, all these they called the latter prophets.

The Jewish Day.

There were two sorts of days amongst the Jews—the natural, which is the space of twenty-four hours, from one sun-set to another; and the civil, or artificial, consisting of twelve hours, from the rising to the setting of the sun, which was divided into four parts, each of which consisted of three hours; they also divided their nights into four parts, which they called watches.

The 1st was the evening.

The 2d the middle, or midnight.

The 3d the cock crowing, from midnight till three in the morning.

The 4th is the morning, or break of day.

Jewish Children taught various Trades.

It was a custom among the Jews, of what rank or quality soever, to teach their children some ingenious craft or art, not only as a remedy against idleness, but as a reserve in time of want. Josephus relates an instance of this custom in the two brothers, Chasinai and Chanilai, who, though they were persons of note, were nevertheless put with a weaver to learn the trade, which, says the historian, was no disparagement to them. Rabbi Jose was a currier; Rabbi Jochanan, was a shoe maker, and from thence surnamed Sandalar.

Jews and Samaritans.

The difference between the Jews and Samaritans, in point of religion, may be reduced to these three heads :—

1. That they looked upon the temple of Gerizim as the only place which God was pleased to be worshipped in, and as the centre of true religion.

2. That they received none other scriptures but the Pentateuch.

3. That their worship had some tincture of paganism, and of the opinions of the nations with whom they conversed.

The Sanhedrim.

This assembly consisted of seventy-one, or seventy-two persons, over whom were two presidents, the chief whereof was generally the high priest, though it was not necessary he should always be so; the other was named the *Ab*, or father of the council; most of the members were priests and levites. Their manner of sitting, was in a semicircle; all matters of importance,' whether ecclesiastical or civil, were brought before this tribunal. The term Sandhedrim, was formed from the Greek συνεδριον which signifies an assembly of people sitting.

Proselytes.

There is frequent mention of proselytes in the New Testament :—

"They were heathens that had embraced the jewish religion. There were two sorts of them; some were called proselytes of habitation, or of the gate, because they were permitted to live within their gates. They were only obliged to forsake idolatry, and to observe the seven precepts which the Talmudists pretend God gave to Adam. Of this kind of proselytes are supposed to have been Naaman the Syrian; the Eunuch of Candace, Queen of Ethiopia; Cornelius; Nicholas, of Antioch; and others mentioned in the Acts; they were not looked upon as Jews."

"The others were called proselytes of the covenant, because they were received by circumcision, which was named, the blood of the covenant; because they were bound to observe the ceremonial law. There were three ceremonies performed at their admission; the first, circumcision; the second, baptism, which was done, by dipping the whole body of the proselyte in water; the third, was a sacrifice, generally of two turtle doves, or two young pigeons; when he had gone through these ceremonies, he was looked upon as a new born babe, he received a new name, and was thenceforward reckoned a Jew."—Maimonides de Proselyt.

Baptism of the Jews.

" The origin of the ceremony of baptism, as used by
the Jews to their proselytes, is entirely unknown. The
Rabbies will have it to be of very ancient date ; some
carry it up to the time of Moses. St. Paul seems to
have been of the same opinion, when he saith the
Israelites were baptized unto Moses. The baptism
of proselytes, may, however, be more properly said to
have owed its rise to the Pharisees. It is manifest
from the gospels, that it was usual for the Jews to
admit men to the profession of a doctrine by baptism ;
for the Pharisees do not find fault with John's baptism,
but only blame him for baptizing, when he was neither
the Messiah, nor Elias, nor that Prophet.

" The proselytes were baptized in the presence of
three persons of distinction, who stood as witnesses.
The proselyte was asked, whether he did not embrace
that religion upon some worldly view? Whether he
was fully resolved to keep the commandments of God?
And whether he repented him of his past life and
actions ?"—Beausobre's Introd. to the New Testament.

The Phylactery.

Phylactery is a Greek word, that signifies a memorial, or preservation. The Hebrew name for phylac-
teries, is tephillim, which signifies prayers ; because
the Jews wore them chiefly when at prayers. They
were long and narrow pieces of parchment, formed
with great nicety, whereon were written thirty pas-

D

sages out of Exodus and Deuteronomy, which they tied to their foreheads and left arms, in memory of the law.

The Feast of the Passover.

The guests leaned on their left arms upon beds round a table, on which was set a lamb, with bitter herbs, unleavened bread, and a dish full of a kind of sauce, or thick mixture, wherein they dipped their bread and herbs; this the Jews called charosset, in remembrance of the mortar they had used, when making bricks in Egypt. They made it at first with dates, and dried figs, but the modern Jews make it of chesnuts, apples, &c. The Talmudists pretend that the reclining posture was then absolutely necessary; as a fit emblem of that rest and freedom, which God had granted to the children of Israel, by bringing them out of Egypt; but it was very common among the eastern nations, to lie on beds when they took their meals, as is evident from sacred as well as profane history.

Feast of Tabernacles.

The feast of tabernacles lasted seven days. It was instituted by God for a memorial of the Israelites having dwelt in tents, or tabernacles, while they were in the desert; they were obliged during the whole solemnity to dwell in tents. One of the most remarkable ceremonies was, the libations, or pouring out of the water, which was performed every day:—a priest went and drew some water at the pool of Siloam, and carried it into the temple, where he poured it on the altar, the people singing, in the mean time, these words, out of the prophet Isaiah, "*with joy shall ye draw water out of the wells of salvation.*" Jesus Christ manifestly alluded to it, when on the last great day of the feast, he cried out, "If any man thirst, let him come unto me, and drink." On the seventh day, they went seven times round the altar, and this was called the great Hosanna.

The Sadducees.

The sect of the Sadducees derived its name from Sadok, a pupil of Antigonus Sochæus, president of the Sanhedrim, or great council, who flourished about two hundred and sixty years before the christian era; and who inculcated the reasonableness of serving God disinterestedly, and not under the servile impulse of the fear of punishment, or the mercenary hope of reward. Sadok, misunderstanding the doctrine of his master, deduced the inference that there was no future state of rewards or punishments. Their principal tenets were the following :—

First.—That there is no resurrection, neither angel, nor spirit, and that the soul of man perishes together with the body.

Second.—That there is no fate, or providence, but that all men enjoy the most ample freedom of action ; in other words, the absolute power of doing either good or evil, according to their own choice : hence they were very severe judges.

Third.—They paid no regard whatever to any tradition, adhering strictly to the letter of scripture, but preferring the five books of Moses to the rest.

The Pharisees.

The Pharisees were the most numerous, distinguished, and popular sect among the Jews. The time when they first appeared is not known, but it is supposed to have been not long after the institution of the Sadducees, if indeed, the two sects did not gradually spring up together. They derived their name from the Hebrew word *Pharash,* which signifies separated or set apart, because they separated themselves from the rest of the Jews to superior strictness in religious observances; they boasted, that, from their accurate knowledge of religion, they were the favourites of heaven; and thus, trusting in themselves that they were righteous, despised others.

They ascribed all things to fate, or providence, yet not so absolutely as to take away the free-will of man, though fate does not co-operate in every action. They also believed in the existence of angels and spirits, and in the resurrection of the dead; but, from the account given of them by Josephus, it appears that their notion of the immortality of the soul, was the Pythagorean metempsychosis: that the soul, after the dissolution of one body, winged its flight into another; and that these removals were perpetuated and diversified, through an infinite succession; the soul animating a sound and healthy body, or being confined in a deformed and diseased frame, according to its conduct in a prior state of existence.

The Scribes.

The profession of the Scribes, as they were doctors, was to write copies of the law, to keep it correct, and to read and explain it to the people. This afterwards gave rise to the Masorites, that is, those who criticised upon the letter of scripture, upon the number of verses, words, letters, and points.

The Galileans.

The Galileans spoke an unpolished and corrupt dialect of the Syriac, compounding and using *ain* for *aleph*; *càph* for *beth*; *tau* for *daleth*: and also frequently changing the gutturals. This probably proceeded from their great communication and intermixture with the neighbouring nations. It was this corrupt dialect that led to the detection of Peter, as one of Christ's disciples. The Galileans are repeatedly mentioned by Josephus as a turbulent and rebellious people, and upon all occasions ready to disturb the Roman authority; they were particularly forward in an insurrection against Pilate himself.

Origin of Heresies.

The Jews coming out of the synagogue, brought the same spirit into the church: the different sects among them, proved so many seeds of discord. The Sadducees were not easily brought to believe the resurrection; the Pharisees being extremely zealous for the ceremonial law, and their own traditions, could not but give the christian religion some tincture of this zeal ; the heathens, on the other hand, that had been brought up in the schools of the philosophers, introduced into the christian institution, the subtilties of the Platonic philosophy. In those early times there was no canon of the books of the New Testament, and all instruction was delivered *viva voce* ; even after the canon had been compiled, some difficult passages gave rise to different notions and sects ; add to this, some persons took the liberty of forging Gospels as they thought fit.

Portrait of a Jewish Scribe.

From Dr. Henderson's Biblical Researches, and Travels in Russia.

" Having expressed a wish to obtain some Hebrew manuscripts, my jewish guide conducted me down a narrow lane, to a house of a sopher, or scribe, whose employment consists in multiplying written copies of the law, according to the established rules of the Hebrew calligraphy. His small apartment presented quite a novel scene to my view—on the table before him, lay developed an accurate exemplar, from which he was taking his copy ; rolls of parchment were lying about in every direction ; the walls were hung with compasses, ink bottles, and other implements ; and, in one corner of the room, a number of skins were in a process of preparation, for the use to which they were to be appropriated. As I entered, he looked up, with

all that absence and discomposure which generally
characterizes those who are abruptly roused from the
absorption connected with deep study, or occupied
about some objects requiring the application of profound attention. Some remarks, however, on the nature of his occupation, interspersed with a few technical
phrases in Hebrew, soon excited his curiosity; and,
laying aside his pen, he readily entered into a conversation respecting his business, and the difficulties
inseparable from its proper and conscientious execution.
Unlike other employments, that of a jewish copyist
absolutely and religiously excludes all improvements.
He is tied down to perform every part of the work
exactly as it was done twelve or thirteen centuries ago,
at the period of the composition of the Talmud; to the
laws of writing prescribed in which, he must rigidly
conform, even in the smallest minutiæ. The skins to
be converted into parchment must be those of clean
animals, and it is indispensable that they should be
prepared by the hands of Jews only. Should it be
found that any parts have been prepared by a Goi,
(a name by which Christians, and all who are not Jews,
are designated), it is immediately thrown away, as unfit
for use. When ready, they are cut even, and joined
together by means of thongs made of the same material;
they are then regularly divided into columns, the
breadth of which must never exceed half their length.
The ink employed in writing the law, generally consists
of a composition made of pitch, charcoal and honey;
which ingredients are first made up into a kind of
paste, and after having remained some time in a state
of induration, are dissolved in water, with an infusion
of galls. Before the scribe begins his task, and after

every interruption, he is required to compose his mind,
that he may write under a sensible impression of the
sanctity of the words he is transcribing. Particular
care is taken that the letters be all equally formed; and
so supreme is the authority of antiquity, that where
letters are found in the exemplar, of a larger or smaller
size than the rest, or such as are turned upside down,
or suspended above the line, or where a final shaped
letter occurs in the middle of a word, these blunders
are to be copied with as great fidelity as any part of the
text. Is it not passing strange, that even christian
editors of the Hebrew Bible should have servilely
followed these Jewish peculiarities? It is well known
what importance the genius of rabbinical superstition
has attached to such anomalies; and it is a fact, that
many of them are interpreted in a manner highly re-
proachful to the religion of Christ. For instance, in
Psalm lxxx. 14, the word מיער, ' from the woods,' is
written and printed מיׄער, with the letter *ain* suspended,
because it is the initial of the word עץ, ' tree,' and is
explained, by the Jews, of the cross; while the wild
boar referred to in the context, they blasphemously interpret, of our blessed Saviour; yet this error of transcription is printed in the editions of Opitius, Michaelis,
Vander Hooght, Frey, Leusden, and Jahn, although
corrected in Menasseh Ben Israel's edition of 1635!

" Faults that creep in during transcription may be
rectified, provided it be done within the space of thirty
days; but if more time has elapsed, the copy is declared
to be posel, or forbidden: a word (פסיל) used in scripture to denote a graven image, which the Israelites
were taught to hold in utter detestation. Should
Aleph-Lamed, (אל) or Jod-Hê, (יה) be wrongly written,

it is unlawful to correct or erase them, because they form the sacred names; nor is it permitted to correct any of the divine names, except when they are applied in an inferior · sense; of this, an instance occurs Gen. iii. 5, where the name אלהים Elohim is used twice. The Rabbins regarding it as employed the second time to denote false objects of worship, permit its erasure; but prohibit it at the beginning of the verse, as being undeniably used of the true God. When transcribing the incommunicable name יהוה, Jehovah, the scribe must continue writing it until it be finished, even though a king should enter the room; but if he be writing two or three of these names combined, such as יהוה אלהי צבאות. Jehovah God of Hosts, he is at liberty, after having finished the first, to rise and salute his visitant. Nor is the copyist allowed to begin the incommunicable name immediately after he has dipped his pen in the ink; when he is approaching it, he is required to take a fresh supply, when proceeding to write the first letter of the preceding word.

" Shackled by canons of such exquisite minuteness, it cannot be matter of surprise that the Dubno scribe should exhibit an emaciated appearance, and affix a high price to the productions of his pen. For a copy of the law, fairly written in small characters, he asked ten louis d'ors, and assured me that he had been sometimes paid at the rate of fifty. To the intrinsic value and spiritual beauty of the law of the Lord, he appeared totally insensible!"

Jewish Library burnt.

The Jews in Bevis Marks, formerly possessed a
library of considerable value in their synagogue, relating
to their ceremonials and talmudical worship; but
some narrow minds among them, conceiving, that if
these books should get into the hands of Christians,
they would be disgraced by shameful translations,
agreed among themselves to cause them to be burnt,
for which purpose they employed some of their scribes,
or tephillim writers, to examine into the correctness of
the copies; and receiving a report agreeable to their
wishes, they had them conveyed to Mile End, where
they were all destroyed in a kiln, for it is contrary to
their maxim ever to make waste paper of the sacred
language.

PART III.

Arabic Literature.

This language may be justly designated as sublime, comprehensive, copious, energetic, delicate, majestic, equally adapted for the poignancy of satire, for the mournfulness of elegy, or the grandeur of heroics, for the simplest taste, or the boldest effort of rhetoric. In every stile of composition, the books in this language are numerous, many of them of high intrinsic worth; their books, however, and their language remain still but imperfectly known in Europe, nor can we ever hope for much advancement, until the fancied formidable difficulties of the study are removed; till curiosity is stimulated by a hope of success; till attention is fixed by a conviction of its utility.

It has long been a desideratum, that the historical works of the Arabs, should be placed within the reach of the generality of readers, instead of being inaccessible even to the greater number of orientalists. The fact is, that the manuscripts which remain in the original language, are dispersed in the great libraries; so that it is difficult to procure copies of them, and still more difficult to collect and collate those copies.

The love of knowledge, has now wholly deserted the Mussulman mind, and we only know of what the genius of Arabia has been capable, from the dusty treasures of our libraries ; which we, forgetful of our great benefactors, and proud of our superior affluence, never pause to examine, and rarely condescend to praise.

When I observe how rich the Bodleian Library is in Arabic manuscripts, I am surprised that no one, out of its numerous students, has attempted to give from them, an intelligent history of Arabian literature and science.

· The Arabs, even before Mahomet, were nationally, and habitually orators in their public assemblies, but it was the eloquence of natural talent, mental vivacity, and excited feeling.

The Arabian Nights.

It has been surmised, that the Arabian Nights' Entertainments may have proceeded from the old Pehlevi stock, and from that have been translated into Arabic. It is not improbable, the land of the fairies, the region of the genii, and the king of these imaginary domains, Gian—Ben Gian—are purely Persian ; and so much so, that the first part of Firdousi's epic, Shah Nameh, introduces them to our attention ; but the conception of the eastern genii, seems referrible to a still older source—to the ancient Chaldeans.

𝔚riting.

The Ásiatics in general, begin their manscripts on what we make the last page, and conclude where our books begin. It may be observed also, they never divide a word in writing, by putting some syllables in one line, and the rest in that which follows ; but in order to keep all the lines of an equal length, to which they are exceedingly attentive, they either extend the final, and sometimes the medial letters, by a dash of the reed, with which they write, or when too long, place those letters, which the line will not conveniently hold, on the tops of the others towards the end, in a manner that it cannot be imitated by types, as may be observed in almost every manuscript, but more particularly among the poets.

Library of 𝔐. Langles.

The library of the late M. Langlès was very extensive, and even more select than numerous. In oriental literature it was superior to any private collection in Europe. In every principal city of Europe, he had a bookseller, who had orders to send him every thing that appeared connected with oriental literature. His situation, as administrator of the Royal Library at Paris, and Persian professor, afforded him great facilities ; whenever a curious MS. was rejected from the library, for want of funds, M. Langlès purchased the work ; it was in this way he became possessed of the unique copy of the Ayeen Akbery, the only complete one known to be in existence ; it is the identical copy made by the vizier, for the Emperor himself. The statistical tables alone, would take years to transcribe. An English merchant and his sons were once introduced to M. Langlès, who shewed them this MS. as a great curiosity, and observed, that he had given above one thousand pounds for it : "Bless me," said young Bill-book, "it costs him above fifty pounds a year, at five per cent. interest, and perhaps he does not look at it once a month." There was no answering Cocker's demonstration of the folly of fine books.

Oriental Literature.

The vast stores of the Royal Library at Paris, so rich in oriental literature, are to be explored anew, and those manuscripts deemed worthy of impression, are to be printed at the public expense.

The Syrian Christians.

The value of these Syrian Christians has not been duly appreciated ; they not only planted christianity in India, so firmly, that we have recently found it there, a thousand years after its introduction ; but by their taste and labours, much of the Grecian literature and science had been translated into Syriac, a language which has so much affinity to the Arabic, as to be easily acquired by an Arabian student, and to invite him to the effort.

The best account we have of the Syrian Christians, and their authors, is in the Bibliotheca of Assenanni. It contains curious documents of their activity in diffusing christianity in India, and even China, in the seventh and eighth centuries. To the first volume, a catalogue of the Syrian manuscripts, placed in the Vatican Library by Clement II. is added. Some Arabian Poems are among them.

" That the Syrians were the tutors of the Arabs, may be known by the fact, that many of the Greek mathematicians were translated first into Syriac, and afterwards into Arabic."—Sharon Turner.

Persian Language and Literature.

As closely allied to the Arabic, it may not be uninteresting to give a few notices of Persian literature. The Persian language, for sweetness and harmony, has been compared to the Italian; and for colloquy, it is said to rival the French.

When we consider, that in the general dearth of literature, this nation possessed authors of genius and repute, that the few books which escaped the savage hands of the Saracens, might have likewise perished in the general wreck of Grecian and Roman literature; in such a case, we cannot but admit, that the only knowledge which we could have acquired, must have been from Persia and Arabia; our taste would then have been formed on different materials, and we might, possibly, have despised the beauties we now admire; we have, however, fortunately escaped this calamity. It may be further urged in favour of the Persians, that at the time when literature was secluded from the western world, when the time of our ancestors was employed in ridiculous crusades, and in mitigating the bulls which were fulminated against them, men of science and genius were patronised and rewarded by the sovereigns of Asia. When our barons and nobles were unable to sign their names, Firdousee wrote. But the sun of eastern learning has set for ever, while the one which irradiates our western sky, shines with increasing splendour.

There is a great difference between the Persian spoken in India, and in Persia. The language of the Persians is wonderfully laconic, while that spoken in India, is ridiculously verbose.

Persian Authors.

The fame of a Persian author rests very frequently on the affectation of his style, and the absurdity of his metaphors; he writes to be admired; and the opportunity of adding another jingle to his sentence, could not be missed, though he were to set reason and sense at defiance. Their prose is much more difficult than their poetry; their historical works are written in a very inflated style. Timour Shah took uncommon pains in composing, correcting, and revising, the history of his reign: indeed it appears from Shurf ood Deen's own account, that he was little more than the transcriber of the king's own sentiments; this arose from the circumstance, that most of the historians lived in the court, and under the protection of the prince, whose actions they celebrated.

Persian Style.

As a specimen of their style, the following extract from the Goolistan of Sadee, is characteristic.

" In my juvenile days, I recollect I went to a certain street, in the month of July, and gazed on my beloved; the heat parched the mouth, and the hot wind dried up the marrow of the bone. From the frailty of nature, I could not endure the heat of the sun; I embraced the refuge of the shade of a wall; I trusted that some one would mitigate this excessive heat, by giving me some iced water; when suddenly, from the darkness of the portal of a door, a light burst forth, namely, a beauty, whose excellencies even the tongue of eloquence could not detail; she appeared as the morn after a dark night, or as the water of life issuing from obscurity; holding a goblet of iced water in her hand, mixed with sugar; I instantly seized the liquor, and drinking it off became reanimated."

Persian Literature.

The Unwari Sohelee is a work much read in Persia, and is considered to be one of the best productions in the language. The most admired historical works are, Rozut oos Sufa, by Meer Rhoond; and the Hubeeb oos Syr, by his nephew; the Shah Ubas Namu, and the Life of Nadir Shah, by Mirza Mihdee.

The principal biographical works are, the Tuzkeeru oos Shoora, or Lives of the Poets, by Doulat Shah; and the Atush Kudu, a late production on the same subject.

E

The degree of credit which the Persian language possesses in Europe, may be almost solely ascribed to Sir William Jones; and his Commentarii is the only work which gives any notion of the language and literature of the Persians.

The Shah Nameh.

The most stupendous monument of Eastern literature is the Shah Nameh of the poet Firdousee; a work consisting of 60,000 couplets. The poem was composed under the patronage of Mahmood, Sultan of Ghizni, who appears to have been particularly liberal towards learned men. Firdousee lives fresh in the remembrance of the East, though kings have succeeded kings, and dynasties have followed dynasties; and instead of suffering by a lapse of time, his fame rests upon a more solid and durable foundation. His work has become a model for imitation; and although his successors have partly changed his language, they have not dispensed with the assistance of his images and fables. The whole of the poem takes up a period of not less than 3700 years, and is formed upon the History of Persia.

The Odes of Hafiz.

The Odes of Hafiz have been very generally compared to those of Anacreon, or the Lyrical Odes of Horace: they appear to bear a greater resemblance to the Roman than the Grecian poets. The poetry of

Hafiz is simple and unaffected; there is a wildness, and often a sublimity in Hafiz, which is not to be met with in any other Persian poet.

The Persians insist, and we should give them the merit of understanding their own language, that all the odes of their celebrated poets are mystical, and breathe a fervent spirit of adoration to the Supreme Being.

The Arabs.

The Arabs, before the era of Mahommed, were Sabians; the Persians, Magians: who, whether they sought the mediation of the planets and stars, or endeavoured to reconcile moral good and physical evil, by the existence of two opposite principles, appear to have agreed in the immutable and eternal truth of a great first cause. The Sabians are commonly called by travellers, Christians of St. John the Baptist. The Magians, Guebos, Gours, and, on the western side of India, Parsees.

In the most early times, the Arabs prided themselves on the purity and copiousness of their language; the poignancy of their wit; and the unrestrained eloquence of their compositions. Their generosity was unlimited, and the same hospitality (observes an eloquent historian) which was practised by Abraham, and celebrated by Homer, is still renewed in the camp of the Arabs.

The Sabians.

" They believe one God, and pay adoration to the stars, or the angels and intelligences which they sup-

pose reside in them, and govern the world, under the
Supreme Deity. They endeavour to perfect themselves
in the four intellectual virtues, and believe the souls of
wicked men will be punished for 9000 ages, but will
afterwards be received to mercy. They are obliged to
pray three times a day. They have a great respect
for the Temple of Mecca, and the Pyramids of Egypt,
fancying these last to be the sepulchres of Seth, and of
Enoch and Sabi, his two sons, whom they look on as
the first propagators of their religion. At these struc-
tures, they sacrifice a cock and a black calf, and offer
up incense. Besides the book of Psalms, the only
true scripture they read, they have other books, which
they esteem equally sacred, particularly one in the
Chaldee tongue, which they call the book of Seth, and
is full of moral discourses. This sect say, they took
the name of Sabians from the above mentioned Sabi,
though it seems rather to be derived from צבא, or the
host of heaven, which they worship. Travellers commonly call them Christians of St. John the Baptist,
whose disciples they also pretend to be, using a kind of
baptism, which is the greatest mark they bear to christianity. This is one of the religions, the practice of
which Mahomet tolerated."—Sale's Koran.

Mahommedan Religion.

The propagation of the Mahommedan religion,
effected a wonderful change, not only in Asia, but in
Europe ; it contributed nothing, however, to the
advancement of science. The prophet seems to have
inspired his immediate successors, with the necessity

of keeping his disciples in the profoundest state of
ignorance; and to this political motive we may attri-
bute the memorable destruction of the Alexandrian
Library, which served to heat four thousand baths, for
the space of six months.

Haroun al Raschid.

Philosophy and science met a protector in Haroun
al Raschid, the hero of the Arabian Nights, and the
correspondent of Charlemagne; and under the reign
of his youngest son, Al Mamon, it burst forth with
increased splendour; but his memory will not escape
the charge of extreme barbarism, for having destroyed
the original books he procured to be translated.

The Koran.

The Mahommedans dare not so much as touch it,
without being first washed, or legally purified; which,
lest they should do by inadvertence, they write these
words on the cover or label, *" let none touch it but
they who are clean ;"* they read it with great care, and
respect, never holding it below their girdles. They
swear by it; consult it on weighty occasions; carry it
with them to war; write sentences of it on their
banners; adorn it with gold, and precious stones; and
knowingly suffer it not to be in the possession of any
of a different persuasion.

Mahommedan belief of the Scriptures.

The Mahommedans are taught by the Koran, that God, in divers ages of the world, gave revelation of his will, in writing, to several prophets, the whole, and every word of which, it is absolutely necessary for a good moslem, to believe. The number of these sacred books were, according to them, one hundred and four; of which ten were given to Adam, fifty to Seth, thirty to Edris, or Enoch, ten to Abraham; and the other four, being the Pentateuch, the Psalms, the Gospel, and the Koran, were successively delivered to Moses, David, Jesus, and Mahommed; which last being the seal of the prophets, these revelations are now closed, and no more to be expected. All these divine books, except the four last, they agree to be now entirely lost, and their contents unknown; and of those four, the Pentateuch, Psalms, and Gospel have undergone so many alterations and corruptions, though there may possibly be some part of the true word of God therein, yet no credit is to be given to the present copies in the hands of the Jews and Christians.

The Arabic Language.

The Arabian language, one of the most ancient, has had the fate of other living languages which have been spoken through many ages, and by the inhabitants of different provinces and countries, remote from one another. It has gradually undergone such an alteration, that the Arabic spoken and written by Mahommed, may now be regarded as a dead language.

The old Arabic language is, through all the East, just like Latin in Europe, a learned tongue, to be acquired only in colleges, or by the perusal of the best authors.

There is, perhaps, no other language diversified by so many dialects, as that of Arabia ; the pronunciation of one province, differs from that of the other provinces ; letters and sounds are often changed in such a manner, as to produce an entire alteration upon the words.

In Syria and Palestine, no language is to be heard but the Arabic, and yet the Syriac is not absolutely a dead language, but is still spoken in several villages in the Pashalik of Damascus.

The Arabic character, which was anciently in use, but is now entirely lost, was the Kufic ; it seems to have been been the alphabet of the Arabians of Mecca, for the Koran was originally written in Kufic characters. The invention of modern characters, which are very different from the Kufic, is ascribed to a vizier. The Arabians, Persians, and Turks, write Arabic in sets of characters, differing in several particulars from one another. They have also modes of writing for different forms of business, each of which, has its particular name.

The hand writing of the Arabians, in the common business of life, is not legible. The Orientals, however, value themselves on their writing, and have carried the art of making beautiful written characters to high perfection. The Arabians value chiefly a species of elegance, which consists in their manner of joining their letters ; the want of which, makes them dislike the style in which Arabian books are printed in Europe ; they sign their letters with a sort of cypher, to prevent the possibility of their counterfeiting their signature ; their letters are folded an inch in breadth, and their leaves are pasted together at one end ; they cannot seal them, for wax is so soft in hot countries, that it cannot retain an impression.

Education and Schools of the Arabians.

In cities, many of the lowest of the people are taught both to read and write ; the same qualifications are also common among the sheikhs of the desert ; and in Egypt, persons of distinction retain preceptors in their families to instruct their children, and young slaves as appear to possess natural abilities, like children of the family.

In almost every mosque is a school, denominated Mœddrasse, having a foundation for the support of teachers, and the entertainment and instruction of poor scholars. In great towns are likewise other schools, to which people of middle rank send their children, to receive religious instruction, and likewise to learn reading, writing and arithmetic. There are also schools of this sort in the market place ; they are open like shops toward the street ; the noise and appearance of the passengers does not seem to divert the attention of the scholars, who sit before a small desk, and read their lessons aloud, balancing themselves constantly in their seats ; to such a degree does motion appear requisite to rouse, and keep up the attention of the inhabitants of hot countries. No girls attend these schools, they are privately taught by women.

In some great towns of Arabia there are likewise colleges, in which the sciences of astronomy, philosophy, and medicine are taught; in these, the Arabians, though possessed of natural abilities, have, for want of good books and masters, made but little progress.

The interpretation of the Koran, and the study of the ancient history of the Mahommedans, are the principal employment of men of letters. These studies take up much time ; for the student must not only acquire the ancient Arabic, but also make himself familiar with all the commentators of the Koran, the number of whom is very considerable.

In a country like Arabia, where occasions of speaking in public seldom occur, eloquence is a useless accomplishment, and therefore cannot be much cultivated. The Arabians say, however, that they hear great orators in their mosques. As Europeans are not admitted to hear those sermons, it is not possible to give any account of the sacred eloquence of Arabia.

The only theatres for the exercise of profane eloquence, are the coffee houses ; the guests are served with pipes and a cup of coffee. As the Arabians never engage in any game or conversation with one another, they have readers, or orators, who attend in the coffee houses to amuse them ; they are called Mullachs, or poor scholars.

They select chosen passages from some favorite authors, such as the History of Antar ; the Adventures of Rustan Sal, a Persian hero ; or Beber, king of Egypt ; the history of the Ayubites, anciently sovereigns of Arabia ; and the Life of Bahluldan, a buffoon in the court of Haroun Al Raschid. Others, who aspire to the praise of invention, make tales and fables, which they walk about and recite, or deliver discourses upon any subjects they choose.

Arabic Literature.

The unfortunate traveller, Burckhardt, in a letter from Aleppo, addressed to Mr. Hamilton, the secretary of the African Association, makes the following observations.

" I am now so far advanced in the knowledge of Arabic, that I understand almost every thing that is said in common conversation, and am able to make myself understood on most subjects, although sometimes with difficulty. I have made acquaintance with some shiekhs, and some of the first literati among the Turks of Aleppo ; who, from time to time, visit me. I owe this favour principally to Mr. Wilkins's Arabic and Persian Dictionary ; the common manuscript dictionaries or Kamus, being generally very defective. The learned Turks are often very glad to consult Wilkins, and never do it without exclaiming, ' How wonderful, that a Frank should know more of our language than our first Ulemas.' Learning at Aleppo, is in a very low state ; no science, the Turkish Law excepted, is properly cultivated, not even that of Arabic grammar, which is so necessary to the interpretation of the Koran. I am assured by the best authority, that there are now in this town only three men (two Turks and a Christian) who know this , language grammatically. The chief quality of a literary man, is that of getting by heart a great number of verses made upon different occasions, and of knowing the proper opportunity of reciting them ; to this must be added, a knowledge of the different learned significations of one and the same word, and of words which express the same idea ; for example, the word *adjuz*, which in common language means a decrepid old man, has in the learned language about sixty other different significations ; and there are in Arabian poetry, about one hundred and fifty words for wine ; but to interpret passages of difficult grammatical construction, or rationally to amend errors, or even to compose prose or verse free from grammatical blunders, is a task much above the capacity of an Aleppine Ulema."

In another letter from the same place, he says

" My long stay in Syria, having been determined upon in consequence of the absolute necessity of my familiarising myself with the idiom of these countries, I shall deem it my duty to send you, from time to time, some vouchers of my application to Arabic literature. I have, for some time past, been engaged in an Arabic exercise, which has proved of great utility to me ; it is the metamorphosis of the well known novel of Robinson Crusoe into an Arabian tale, adapted to eastern taste and manners. A young Frank, born at Aleppo, who speaks like a Native, but neither reads nor writes it, has been my assistant in the undertaking. I take the liberty of sending you here inclosed a copy of this travestied Robinson, or, as I call the book in Arabic, Dur el Baheer—the pearl of the seas."

Arabic Manuscripts.

" The library of the convent of Mount Sinai, contains a vast number of Arabic manuscripts and Greek books; the former are of little literary value; of the latter, I brought away two beautiful Aldine editions, a Horace, and an Anthology. The priests would not show me their Arabic memorandum books, previous to the fifteenth century. From those I saw, I copied some interesting documents concerning the former state of the country, and their quarrels with the Bedouins."

Antar.

"Has certainly every characteristic of an epic poem; it is throughout of high interest, and often sublime. I have attentively read little more than one twelfth part of it. The copy I bought at Aleppo, is among the manuscripts which I sent to England, from Syria. The style is very remarkable; without descending to the tone of common conversation, as the one thousand and one nights often do, it is simple and natural, and clear of that bombast, and those forced expressions, and far fetched metaphors, which the orientalists admire, even in their prosaists; but which can never be to the taste of an European critic. I believe Sir William Jones was the first to call the attention of the public to this romantic poem, in his Comment. Poes. Asiat. He possessed only one or two volumes of it."

Study of Arabic.

" By the present opportunity, I transmit to Sir Joseph Banks my journal in the peninsula of Sinai, and to you a volume of proverbs and popular sayings, current at Cairo. I am afraid the committee will be startled at all the Arabic it contains, and exclaim, that the writer was sent to these countries, not to become a translator, but a discoverer. I can assure you I have derived essential benefit from this compilation, while, at the same time, I hope that a knowledge of the Arab nation, and of their present language, may be somewhat advanced by it, and facilitated to others. In translating and explaining these sayings, I wished to leave a memorial with my employers, as well as with the public, that I had acquired a competent knowledge of the vulgar dialect of the people, whom I have described in my journals."

Education among the Nubians.

The few Nubians who know how to write, and who serve the governors in the capacity of secretaries, are taught by the Fokaro of Damer, south of Goos, who are all learned men, and travel occasionally to Cairo. On their way thither, they alight at the houses of the rich inhabitants, and teach their children to read and write. Many of the children of Sukkot, are likewise sent to the school of the Arabs Sheyga, where they remain for ten years and upwards, and are fed and taught gratuitously by the Ulema of that tribe.

History of Nubia.

The best Arabian historian of Nubia, is Iber Selym el Assouary; but I never saw his book either in Syria,

or Egypt. There are also details of the History of
Nubia, in the History of the City of Béhnese, (Oxyrin-
chus) sent to England by Burckhardt.

———————

Burckhardt says, that " numbers of pilgrims, after
having learned to read and write a little, proceed to
Mecca, 'in order to study the Koran and Commen-
taries ; and it is their belief that they can never forget
a chapter which they have once learned in the Beit
Ullah—the House of God."

Mode of Education among the Malays in Penang.

There is no fixed standard as to ages ; all are admitted
from six years old and upwards, just as circumstances
may direct. The parents at the time they deliver up
a child to the master, offer a small present of planta-
tions, tobacco, &c. Sometimes, when they can afford
it, a rupee or a dollar. They then say to the master,
" this child we entirely surrender to you ; he is not
now ours but yours ; we only ask for his eyes and
limbs ; and that he may not be crippled, or severely
wounded in chastisement." In every other respect he
is solely at the disposal of the teacher.

After these ceremonies, the child is regularly received
by the master into the school, and entitled to all the
advantages of the institution.

When a boy has gone through the Koran, which is
considered as a kind of finish to his education, his
parents give sedekah, or alms ; which, in this instance,
has a special reference to what is given exclusively for

instruction. The parents reward the teacher according to their ability; the rich will give from twenty to seventy dollars, and upwards; and if they consider the master as having done his duty, frequently add a new turban, a gown, and a piece of white cloth. A feast sometimes follows, when a company of old men are invited, who are supposed to know the Koran well; the boy is called into the presence of these old men, and his master, when, with an audible voice, he is ordered to read a chapter or two from the Koran; after which the judgment of the old men, which is mostly favourable, stamps dignity on the teacher as being very learned.

In many cases, however, the schoolmaster does not succeed so well; and not unfrequently fails to obtain any emolument whatever, from parents whose children he has instructed. The custom of paying nothing till the education of the children is completed, often proves very injurious to the teacher.

In case the father dies, or becomes very poor, the master either loses the expected reward, or has great difficulty in obtaining it; it being perfectly optional with the parents, whether they give any thing, or not; extreme poverty is always considered a sufficient excuse. Very poor people can take their children to a Mahommedan teacher for instruction; and should he refuse, or ask for wages, he is liable to be disgraced—he is obliged to receive them. The Islams say, that all good teachers, who fear God in truth, will not, dare not, ask for any recompense for instructing the ignorant.

SCHOOL HOURS.—It will appear that the poor schoolmaster has plenty to do. The schools open in the morning at seven o'clock, and close at eleven ; when the children go home to eat rice. At two o'clock the schools are reopened, and the children read till five ; when the master's ordinary work for the day is done. ᵗ The time also of continuance in school is quite uncertain ; some boys who are of very bright intellect, will go through the Koran in one year ; but many require a much longer space of time, and some even in ten years do not finish the book. The children receive no rewards whatever for making progress in learning ; on the contrary, their punishments are very severe.

MODE OF TEACHING.—The boys are first taught the Arabic alphabet, which is mostly written on a board for that purpose ; when they know all the cha- racters, the Koran is put into their hands, and they read a chapter which treats on prayer ; but if the teacher does not explain the same to them, they are just as wise when they have read the chapter, as they were before ; and as the Koran is in the Arabic tongue, the teacher himself is frequently unable to explain it. Great numbers read the Koran who are not able to explain a single chapter. It is the principal book read in the Mahommedan schools ; nothing more is taught, unless the teacher is desired to do so by the parents. In some instances the children continue at school after they have read the Koran, when they proceed to Al Kitab, or the book which explains the doctrines and ceremonies of Islamism, and is con- sidered by some an explanation of the Koran.

This may be viewed as one of the means employed for propagating Mahommedanism. Five leading tenets are principally insisted upon, and care is taken to impress the minds of the children with the importance

of them; and frequently these doctrines are interspersed
with the regular lessons of the day. It is no uncommon thing, when passing the schools, to hear the
children singing praises to all the prophets; and they
are thus supposed to have made considerable progress
in their learning.

Writing is also taught in the native schools, as soon
as the boys can read with tolerable facility. They
commence by writing the characters on boards, which,
when full, are washed, and used again, and again; and
so they proceed by degrees to the use of paper, and
write what the master may order. In seventeen schools
there were only three in which the Malay language,
formed a branch of the regular course.

Mahommedan Negroes at Kamalia.

Mungo Park, says the schoolmaster at Kamalia,
possessed, exclusive of the Koran, a variety of manuscripts, which had partly been purchased from the
trading Moors, and partly borrowed from Bushreens
in the neighbourhood, and copied with great care;
on interrogating the schoolmaster, I discovered that
the negroes are in possession of an Arabic version of
the Pentateuch, which they call (Tàureta el Moosa);
this is so highly esteemed, that it is often sold for the
value of one prime slave. They have likewise a version of the Psalms of David, and lastly the book of
Isaiah, and it is in very high esteem;. I suspect,
indeed, that in all these copies there are interpolations
of some of the peculiar tenets of Mahommed; for I
could distinguish in many passages the name of the

F

Prophet. By means of these books many of the negroes have acquired an acquaintance with some of the remarkable events recorded in the Old Testament.

Eastern Mode of Education.

We may, perhaps, gain some notion of the ancient mode of teaching, from the present method adopted by the Malays, at Malacca.

The regular time for entering school is at the age of seven, when the boy enters the school room, he prostrates himself, and embraces the master's feet ; the master recites fatihat—the first chapter in the Koran.

The period at school depends upon circumstances. The Malays do not write upon sand like the Malabars. For paper they use a thin board, made of a very light wood, called puley, with a fine grain, and rubbed over with white wash made of pipe clay ; for pens they use a hollow reed, or the kalam of the sago tree. Their ink is made of rice, burnt over the fire till it is quite black, and when pounded, fine pure water is put on it, and then it is strained through a cloth. They use the Arabic characters. The boy begins with writing the alphabet on the board, at the top of which they never omit to write

بسم الله الرحمن الرحيم

In the name of the merciful and gracious God.

When the board is full they go to the well, and wash all clean off. The Koran is exclusively taught in the school, in Arabic ; and without explanation. The children sit flat on the ground, or flooring, in a hut

covered with the attap leaf. The morning begins with
a new lesson ; in the afternoon they repeat what they
have learned, which exercise is called صندارس
mendras, ready off ; then they write—the beginners the
alphabet, the more advanced copy out of the Koran ;
thus they learn the whole of the Koran from the board
by piecemeal.

Hariri.

Hariri, who lived in the 446th year of Hegira,
developed all the richness of his language, in a happy
melange of prose and verse ; containing stories always
agreeable ; full of antitheses, and play upon words ;
his harmonious and rich language, presents to those
who are desirous of translating it, difficulties that are
almost insurmountable. These difficulties, however,
have not deterred several German, English, and
Spanish authors, who have made Hariri's work known
to us by extracts. A Jew among them, published a
Hebrew translation, under the title, Méchaberot Ithiel.

Mode of Education among the Chinese.

The children, when they first enter school, have to
gain the first rudiments of knowledge in a language
they have hitherto, in a great measure, been unacquainted with ; dark, dreary, and toilsome is the journey
they have to pursue through an immense labyrinth of
difficult and uncouth characters, and harsh and unusual

sounds, without one single ray of light to direct their steps, or reward their toils, the difficulties of which are heightened by the unsystematic method of education.

Fifteen years ago, at Malacca there were eight Chinese schools, containing about one hundred and fifty scholars; of this number scarcely one in ten continue long enough to derive any essential benefit from the school; the poorer class cannot afford to keep their children at school longer than two or three years, during which time they are scarcely able to learn any thing useful, having only time to get the first rudiments; and being taken from school at an early period, before they have learnt to apply their acquisitions to practical uses, all that they have gained is soon forgotten.

CEREMONIES ON ENTRANCE.—It is customary on this occasion, for the scholar to bring a few articles as a present to the master, among which are, an egg, and a cup of dried pulse; the one indicating the clearness of intellect necessary for learning, and the other implying a wish, that the master's instructions may flow with ease into the scholar's mind, as the pulse flows from the cup when it is inverted. In China the scholars provide even the master's clothes.

At the head of the school there is generally an altar piece, with the words, " The ancient teacher Confucius, who has eminently attained the rank of the most holy sage, or, the teacher and pattern for myriads of ages." written in large characters; an incense pot is placed before it, and candles are kept constantly burning on the altar. The scholar on his first entrance must bow before this altar, as also every day on coming to school. This is considered not merely as a tribute of respect to the deceased sage, but as an act of worship to him as a demi-god.

SCHOOL MONEY.—The average sum paid as school money, is, for the poorer children, about eight dollars a year ; the rich give double that sum, and often more than double, according to their ability, and the care they wish to be taken of their children ; in addition to this, the parents provide the children with books, ink, ink-stones, paper, pencil, tables, and stools, and every thing requisite for a school, except the bare apartment. The school money is paid at the end of the year, and a whole year's school money is expected, whether the children attend the full time or not. The schoolmaster's stipend is called, in polite language, Sew-kin, regulated gold.

SCHOOL HOURS.—These are, from six in the morning, until six in the evening ; allowing two or three hours in the morning, and at noon, for meals ; in the evening, the scholars attend to their lessons at home, that they may bring them perfect the next day.

Their holidays are not numerous ; they consist merely of the four feasts at the four seasons of the year, various other feasts, and the birth day of Confucius. The schools break up about the twelfth month, and do not re-open till about the middle of the first month of the ensuing year.

MODE OF EDUCATION.—Reading. The scholars read aloud, both when studying, and repeating their lessons ; in this each one seems to strive to outvie the other in noise, which in a school containing thirty or forty children is extremely loud, and may be heard at a great distance. The first book they commence with, is the San-tze-king, or the three character classic ; a book which has nothing more to recommend it for the use of children, than that it is written in a sort of rhyme; but the style of which is difficult, and the subject, in some parts, abstruse and distant from their thoughts ; they of course do not understand it, neither is it the care of the teacher to make it intelligible to them. When they have committed this little book to memory, which, though it contains but one thousand and fifty six monosyllabic words, yet takes many of them six months, and some a whole year, they then proceed to the four books of Confucius ; these they first read over, and afterwards commit to memory, without having a single character explained to them ; they labour early and late at this toilsome task, and yet it is four or five years before they can accomplish it. When the four books are finished, they then begin the commentary on them, written by Choo-foo-tze, and commit that likewise to memory. Having arrived at this period of their studies, the teacher begins to explain to them something of what they have been learning for the last five years, and to make it a little intelligible to them ; to do this sooner is considered by the teachers to be but lost labour, as the children are not till then capable of understanding, and appreciating their instructions. The work of the teacher being now increased, his salary must also be raised ; otherwise the unfortunate scholars are likely to continue in the same state of darkness and ignorance. After the four books, with the commentary on them, are finished, the scholar next proceeds to the Woo-king, a very ancient composition, and very difficult to understand. Having passed through this series of studies, the young man is considered as " paou keoh," *i. e.* " having a bellyful of learning," ánd is sent out ínto the _world to do for himself.

The practice of committing to memory whatever they learn, is of great importance in Chinese, and would be extremely useful, were the teachers but to explain the meaning of the books to the pupils as they go on ; but at present ít is a heavy burden laid on their shoulders, which they find it difficult to bear. Interested motives first gave rise to this useful practice, otherwise it would not perhaps have become so general ; in China, no one can lawfully be raised to any office under the state, who is not able to repeat the sacred books, and to compose some piece on the doctrines contained in them, which undergoes a most rigorous examination.

In schools among the Fokien people, the practice of committing much to memory is not attended with that benefit which might be expected ; from the circumstance of their colloquial dialect, being entirely different from that in which they read and learn, in so much, that though persons may be well acquainted with the colloquial dialect, yet the dialect in which they read is so different, that much may be committed to memory, without its being understood. This forms a great barrier to improvement in Fokien schools, as the scholars have two dialects to acquire, before they can understand, or make themselves intelligible to others. The same is the case in Canton schools.

WRITING THE CHARACTER.—This is a most essential practice for those who study Chinese, as well for natives as foreigners ; the symbols of the language being so numerous, that without constant and unintermitted practice, it is impossible to rivet them in the mind. In Chinese schools this forms a part of every day's labour, but it is not so fully attended to, nor such facilities afforded for it, as the nature of the difficulties to be encountered require. They have copy books, as in European schools, the paper of which being thin, the copies are placed underneath, and the pupil is made to decypher the characters on the upper sheet; but the master does not point out the component parts of the character, nor trouble himself to make the scholar acquainted with the radicals of the language; and no exercise of mind being required in mere copying, the scholar is some time before he begins to think for himself, or can decypher the characters, without the help of the copy. Both in reading and writing the children are taught individually, there being no classes in Chinese schools, by which much advantage is lost, and no laudable emulation excited.

ARITHMETIC.——This is not taught in Chinese schools, the teachers themselves being generally ignorant of it, they consider it rather the business of the shop than the school, where the children must go to learn it.

PUNISHMENT.——The punishments inflicted on the idle and disobedient, vary according to the disposition of the master: they employ the rattan, and a flat piece of bamboo, about an inch broad, and two feet long, which they call a choh-pae; those masters who are more cruel, strike very hard with these, so as even to produce blood; when the scholar has not got his lesson perfect, he is obliged to kneel down, and learn it on his knees; the more incorrigible are made to kneel on gravel and small stones strewed on the floor, or on a couple of cockle shells inverted, to increase the pain. In some instances, fines are exacted on the elder boys, who are more sensible of shame, and the money is appropriated for the purchase of paper, ink, &c. which are distributed among the more deserving ; these fines however, are not imposed in every school, and when they are not, there are no rewards which the deserving can have to look for, except exemption from punishment.

PART IV.

NOTICES OF REMARKABLE LINGUISTS.

JOHN FOWLER HULL.

John Fowler Hall was the son of Samuel Hull, an eminent miller at Uxbridge, and a member of the Society of Friends. At an early age he had a strong desire to go abroad, but the thought of crossing the water to Calais appeared an insuperable obstacle ; he at last overcame his fears, and having obtained the permission of his parents, undertook a journey overland to India with a view of improving his knowledge in some of the Oriental languages, in which he had made a remarkable progress before he left Europe, and had read nearly the whole of the Greek and Latin authors before he left school, which was in his sixteenth year. At the decease of his father he became possessed of a handsome fortune, a great portion of which he expended in his favourite studies, and the purchase of valuable books and manuscripts. To great literary attainments (for his knowledge was by no means confined to languages,) this extraordinary young

man united a simplicity of manners and a goodness
of heart, which will long endear his memory to all
who knew him. He died on the 18th of December,
1825, in his 26th year, after a short illness, at Sigaum,
a small village about forty miles south of Dharwur
in India. He bequeathed all his manuscripts, books,
and papers, to the British Museum, and they are
now deposited in that vast collection.

Amongst the manuscripts, one of his executors
informed me, there were many very curious and
valuable in the Sanscrit, Hindostánee, Arabic, Persian, Chinese, and Malay languages, which he had
collected in his extraordinary pedestrian journey
through India. His manuscript journal would be
highly interesting to the public, and would well re-
pay the visit of an industrious biographer to the
British Museum, in order to the publication of a
more extended memoir of the life and travels of this
singular and most exemplary youth.

THOMAS ZOUCH,

AN UNKNOWN POET AND TEACHER OF LANGUAGES.

Thomas Zouch was born at Saffron Walden, in
Suffolk, in the year 1750; his father was born in
the reign of William and Mary, and was one of the
first clerks to the bank of England, which situation
he held for about forty-five years, and was buried
in Lothbury church-yard, which was afterwards
desecrated for the purpose of increasing the offices
of the bank. Thomas Zouch was educated at Ches-

hunt, under the care of a Mr. Williams, who kept a boarding-school at that place. After various attempts in trade, which proved unsuccessful, he applied himself more sedulously to the acquiring a knowledge of the French language, with a view to gain a livelihood by teaching it. He possessed a remarkably tenacious memory; his company was at all times amusing and instructive, and from his long residence in London, he acquired a fund of anecdote, both political and historical, of his own times.

At the period of the French Revolution he taught the English tongue to a great number of the French emigrant nobility and dignitaries of the Gallican church. Amongst his pupils were the Vicomte Chateaubriand, the Duke de Berri, the Duc de Chartres, with all of whom he was upon terms of the greatest intimacy whilst in this country. Latterly, from his advanced years, he obtained but little employment, though he was remarkably quick and active, and in full possession of all his faculties.

As a resource against the infirmities of old age, he had paid a subscription to a club, for about twenty-three years; during which period, from his uniform excellent state of health, he had never occasion to apply for any assistance.

From the scantiness of his resources he had fallen into arrears for rent, and his landlord demanding immediate payment, he was compelled, to satisfy those demands, to part with all his books, (in number about three hundred volumes,) and philosophical instruments. This proved a severe trial to him, and his health from that time visibly declined.

In his last illness he was compelled to ask relief from his club; when, as the preliminary to such assistance, he was visited by the secretary, who found him sitting up writing a letter to a friend, upon which he thought proper to report him able to get his bread; he was therefore refused all aid, and was entirely dependant upon the bounty of his friends for the common necessaries of life.

On his death, application was made for the sum of thirty pounds, stipulated in the articles, to pay for a decent funeral, which they also, at first, refused; and not until a threat of an appeal to a magistrate, would they make the grant for paying the expences incurred.

I applied for him to the literary fund, but I was informed relief was only afforded to those who had written and published one or more works.

For nearly two years before his death, he had always a plate at my father's table, which he frequently availed himself of, having often not wherewith to purchase a dinner.

He died on the 15th of February, 1823, aged seventy-three, and was buried in St. James's burying-ground, Hampstead Road.

He had a competent knowledge also of the Latin and Greek languages, mathematics, and use of the globes. He had also obtained a great proficiency in the Hebrew and Arabic languages.

He frequently amused his friends with pieces of poetry, of a humourous kind, of his own composition; he has left four volumes of manuscript poems, written at various periods.

For a very curious memoir of an illustrious obscure, who obtained a remarkable proficiency in
languages and mathematical science, I must refer
the reader to my little Gate to the French, Italian,
and Spanish Unlocked.

MUTUAL EDUCATION SOCIETY.

A writer in the Monthly Magazine, for May
1821, communicates the following curious institution for acquiring knowledge in sacred literature.—

A few years since Dr. Spencer, then a resident in
Bristol, conceived the idea of forming an institution
in which the languages of holy writ and scriptural
knowledge should be taught gratuitously, and this
institution he proposed to found upon the following
principles ;—

First—That which a person is competent to learn,
if he be properly instructed, he will be able to
teach.

Second—That after a person has learnt any thing,
it will be highly conducive to his improvement if he
begin to teach it.

Third—That a person will learn more easily
and expeditiously in a class than individually.

Fourth—That it is more pleasant and easy to teach
a class than one alone.

Upon these principles the doctor commenced his
plan, which he denominated an institution for ac-

quiring and communicating an accurate and critical knowledge of the Holy Scriptures in their original languages, free of expence, by taking four young men as students, whom he instructed in their own language grammatically, in rhetoric, logic, the Hebrew of the Old Testament, the Greek of the Septuagint and of the New Testament; besides which the students read with him the History of the Empires with which the Jews were connected, with the customs of the Jews and other eastern nations, Christian ecclesiastical history, &c. &c.

Previously, however, to his taking this class, he obtained from each individual a solemn promise that he would, at the expiration of three years, take other four pupils, and instruct them in all those things which should be taught him in the institution he was then about to enter.

When a student has completed his studies, at the end of three years he takes a class of four, who each engage to teach four others as the last did; and when they have arranged amongst themselves the days and hours of meeting for the week, they proceed to business, which consists in reading

Watts's Logic,
English Testament,
English Grammar,
English Bible,
Scripture Geography,
Rhetoric,
Learning Hebrew Grammar,
Translating Hebrew Bible.

This constitutes the work of the first year; it is, however, by no means necessary that the task should be read a great many times through ; others are sometimes introduced at the discretion of the teachers : thus in a class-book is contained the following arrangement, dated March 3, 1821.

Read—Locke on the Human Understanding, four
  pages.
  English Grammar, two chapters.
  English Bible, two chapters.
  French Testament, seven chapters.
  Hebrew Grammar, four chapters.
  Hebrew Bible, one chapter, and parsed.

This is the business of one evening, in a class which meets twice a week ; the plan requires six hours in the week to be devoted to it, but the division of this time is quite immaterial.

At the expiration of a year from the time of the class commencing, the teacher introduces the Greek language, and the arrangement then is

  Greek Grammar,
  Greek Testament,
  Shuckford and Prideaux,
  Scripture Geography,
  Josephus.
  Septuagint,
  Hebrew Bible,
  English Bible and Testament,
  Locke.

These works are not all introduced at once to the pupils, but in succession. When a work has been read through, the teachers examine the students as to their knowledge of its contents, and if satisfied, introduce another.

The third year is employed in gaining a more complete, correct, and critical knowledge of the Hebrew and Greek languages, in comparison of different passages with each other; and of the Septuagint with the Hebrew.

The increasing character of the plan will be seen in the annexed calculation, where, supposing each individual to have adhered to his engagement, and to have taken his class at the expiration of his term of three years, we shall have

Founder 1
In three years completes
   the education of . . . . 4 students.
Who finish in 6 years . . . 16
           9 64
       12 256
       15 1,024
       18 4,096
       21 16,382
       24 65,536
       27 . . . 262,144
       30 . . . 1048,576

The principles of its future government were,

First—A general meeting of members and teachers to be held annually on the first Tuesday in July, when a committee is to be formed from amongst them by general suffrage, on which day a report of the last committee, and other business of a general nature considered.

Second—All propositions made at the general meeting to be carried by votes. All questions of the committee to be determined by the ballot of the majority.

The business of the committee is to receive reports from the teachers of the progress of their respective classes. To examine into and decide upon the eligibility of persons applying for admission.

The writer says, some of the most distinguished dignitaries of the church have sanctioned this undertaking.

FINIS.

W. DAVY, Printer, Gilbert Street, Grosvenor Square.

POSTSCRIPT.

It is my intention to publish a sheet of verbs, on a plan that will considerably facilitate their acquisition, and likewise some of the particles of each language. I do not pretend to supply the place of a grammar, but merely to shew that, by having cards written out from the various grammars, much time may be saved; and an easier method of acquiring those languages will at once be evident from their affinity to each other.

For the Hebrew—I must recommend the beginner to obtain a sheet of letters and vowels, by which he will more easily acquire the habit of correct pronunciation. Professor Lee's Hebrew grammar must next be procured which contains much valuable information.

There is an excellent grammar by Gesenius, which has not yet been fortunate enough to meet with a translator from the German. Begin early to translate, for which you will find great facilities in the purchase of Montanus's Hebrew Bible, with an interlinear literal translation in the Latin language, which originally formed a part of the Complutensian Polyglot. Hutter's Hebrew Bible has the servile letters printed hollow for the use of learners,

whereby they may at once see the roots of the words.
I do not consider, however, there is much advantage
in this plan.

There is an excellent stereotype edition of the
Hebrew Bible, in one volume 8vo., published by Mr.
Duncan, for 25s.

Bythner's Lyra Prophetica is an excellent book on
the Psalms : there is a new cdition, edited by Dr.
Sleath.

IN LEXICONS—There is an excellent old book by
Avenarius, in folio, 1587; the roots are printed in
large letters on the margin, and the various readings
are given underneath : very useful for a beginner.

That of Buxtorf is remarkable for its extent of
Rabbinical learning, but it is not so well calculated
for a learner.

There is an excellent little pocket manual, by
Reineccius, Leipsic, 1735 ; containing all the Hebrew
roots, entitled, Index Memorialis.

An octavo edition of Gesenius's Hebrew Lexcion,
edited by Gibbs, has just appeared. Gesenius, it must
be observed, has adopted the etymological form, as is
the case with the dictionaries of the modern languages. It is admitted the old method of finding
words by their roots is often very perplexing to a
learner. Gesenius has also admirably illustrated the
use of the Hebrew words, by their affinity to the
Arabic and Syriac. For a learner adopting my
method, I must strenuously recommend this Lexion ;
he will find it invaluable; the price is 25s.; beautifully
printed.

IN ARABIC—The grammar of Richardson is well
known, yet in many respects objectionable and un-

satisfactory: that of Erpenius, though much older, is far superior, in all respects.

Amongst the moderns, none rank so high as that of Silvestre de Sacy, in two vols. 8vo. 1810, 36s.: he is a most profound Arabic scholar. I am surprised we have not had an abridgment of this excellent grammar, done into English.

There is another, by an anonymous author, published in Paris, in 1824, for 21s.; with Exercices d'Arabe litteral, 8vo. 4s. The Lexicon used by the servants of the East India Company, is that of Richardson's, in Persian, Arabic, and English. There is an old one by Willemet, which I understand is reprinting.

I have a curious grammar which belonged to the poor old Cobler, mentioned in the Gate to French, Italian, and Spanish, which is thus entitled, Grammatica—Hebreo—Harmonico cum Arabica et Aramæa Methodo—Logico—J. G. Kals, Amsterdam, 1758. If something on the same plan could be done in this country, it would be a treasure to the biblical student, divested of the absurdities and conceits which depreciate the value of this book: it is, however, very curious, and even entertaining.

For the Syriac—The grammar of Mr. Yeates is the best that can be named. I believe he is preparing a Lexion. There is a good Lexicon attached to an edition of the Syriac New Testament, by Gutbirius, 12mo. 1668. However, the invaluable Lexicon Heptaglotton of Castell, will supply all the wants of the biblical student in this department: it is an honor to this country to have produced such a work; but the poor man was ruined, and died in abject poverty.

In recurring again to the helps for the Hebrew language, I cannot omit noticing the advantage I have derived from a little book by Paul Tossano, called Dictionum Hebraicarum quæ universo sepher tehillim continentur, Syllabus geminus; every word in the Psalms is to be found at the end, alphabetically arranged and numbered, referring to its root, whereby the learner may, without the least difficulty or fear of mistake, translate for himself the whole book of Psalms. Those who are acquainted with Greek, would derive much pleasure from the use of the Concordance, by Conrad Kircher, 2 vol. 4to. 1608, with all the readings of the Greek Septuagint. That of Trommius's is more esteemed, but especially that invaluable book, Taylor's Hebrew Concordance, 2 volumes, folio.

Pl. 1.

Hebrew Alphabet.

Figure	Name	Pronunciation
א	Aleph	
ב	Beth	B often V
ג	Gimel	G hard
ד	Daleth	D
ה	He	H aspirated
ו	Vau	V
ז	Zain	Z
ח	Cheth	Ch { strong aspiration
ט	Teth	T
י	Yood	Y
כ	Caph	K
ל	Lamed	L
מ	Mem	M
נ	Noon	N
ס	Samech	S
ע	A-yin	Guttural Aspiration
פ	Pe & Ph	P & Ph
צ	Tsade	Ts
ק	Koof	K
ר	Resch	R
ש	Sheen & Seen	Sh & S
ת	Tav or Thav	T & Th

Pl. 2.

Arabic Alphabet.

Figure	Name	Pronunciation	Numero
١	Alif	A	1
ب	Ba	B	2
ت	Ta	T	3
ث	Tha	Th	4
ج	Jim	J	5
ح	Hha	H	6
خ	Kha	Kh	7
د	Dal	D	8
ذ	Dhsal	DS	9
ر	Ra	R	10
ز	Za	Z	11
س	Sin	S	12
ش	Shin	Sh	13
ص	Sad	'S	14
ض	Dad	D́	15
ط	Ta	T́	16
ظ	Da	D́	17
ع	Ain	Á	18
غ	Ghain	G	19
ف	Fa	F	20
ق	Kaf	K	21
ک	Kef	K	22
ل	Lam	L	23
م	Mim	M	24
ن	Nun	N	25
و	Waw	W	26
ه	He	H	27
ي	Ye	Y	28

Syriack Alphabet.

Figure	Name	Estrang	Nu...
?	Olaph	?	1
?	Beth	?	2
? ?	Gomal	?	3
?	Dolath	?	4
?	He	?	5
?	Vau	?	6
?	Zain	?	7
?	Hheth	?	8
?	Teth	?	9
?	Jud	?	10
?	Coph	?	20
?	Lomad	?	30
?	Mim	?	40
?	Nun	? ?	50
?	Semkat	?	60
?	Ee	?	70
?	Pee	?	80
?	Tsode	?	90
?	Koph	?	100
?	Rish	?	200
?	Shin	?	
? ?	Thau	?	

Pl. 4.

The Samaritan Alphabet.

Samaritan	Hebrew	Name
ᛉ	א	Aleph
ᔈ	ב	Beth
ᖶ	ג	Gimel
ᔊ	ד	Daleth
ᔈ	ה	He
ᔈ	ו	Vau
ᔈ	ז	Zain
ᔈ	ח	Hheth
ᔈ	ט	Teth
ᔈ	י	Yod
ᔈ	כ	Caph
2	ל	Lamed
ᔈ	מ	Mem
ᔈ	נ	Nun
ᔈ	ס	Samech
▽	ע	Aain
ᒎ	פ	Pe
ᔈ	צ	Tsade
ᔈ	ק	Koph
ᔈ	ש	Shin
ᔈ	ת	Tau

Pl. 5.

Arabic.   *Syriack.*

Final	Medial	Initial	Arabic Names	Final	Medial	Initial	Syriack Names	Heb:
١١	ا	ا	Alif	—	ؤ	ؤ	Olaph	א
ب	ب	ب	Ba	ܒ	ܒ	ܒ	Beth	ב
ج ج	ج	ج	Jim	ܓ	ܓ	ܓ	Gomal	ג
د	د	د	Dal	،	؛	؛	Dolath	ד
ذ	ذ	ذ	Dsal					
ه ه	ه	ه	He	—	ܗ	ܗ	Ha	ה
و	و	و	Wau	—	ܘ	ܘ	Vau	ו
ز	ز	ز	Za	—	ܙ	ܙ	Zain	ז
ح ح	ح	ح	Ha	ܚ	ܚ	ܚ	Hhet	ח
خ خ	خ	خ	Hha					
ط	ط	ط	Tsa	ܛ	ܛ	ܛ	Teth	ט
ظ	ظ	ظ	Tha					
ي ي	ي	ي	Ya	ܝ	ܝ	ܝ	Yood	י
ك ك	ك	ك	Kef	ܟ	ܟ	ܟ	Coph	כ
ل ل	ل	ل	Lam	ܠ	ܠ	ܠ	Lomad	ל
	لا	لا	Lam Elif	ܡ	ܡ	ܡ	Mim	מ
م م	م	م	Mim	ܢ	ܢ	ܢ	Noon	נ
ن ن	ن	ن	Nun					
				ܣ	ܣ	ܣ	Semcat	ס
ع ع	ع	ع	Ain	ܥ	ܥ	ܥ	Ee	ע
غ غ	غ	غ	Ghain					
ف ف	ف	ف	Fa	ܦ	ܦ	ܦ	Phe	פ
ص ص	ص	ص	Sad	ܨ	ܨ	ܨ	Zode	צ
ض ض	ض	ض	Dad					
ق ق	ق	ق	Kaph	ܩ	ܩ	ܩ	Kooph	ק
ر	ر	ر	Ra	—	—	ܪ	Risch	ר
س س	س	س	Sin	*Not in Syriack*				ש
ش ش	ش	ش	Shin	ܫ	ܫ	ܫ	Schin	ש
ت ت	ت	ت	Ta					
ث ث	ث	ث	Thsa	ܬ	ܬ	ܬ	Thau	ת

The Arabic Alphabet has 28 letters, which are usually arranged different from those of the Hebrew, ———— the similar characters are placed together in this Table as they correspond with the Hebrew.

Pl. 6.

Hebrew Vowels.

The Hebrew Language has Ten Vowels.

1. Five long:

(◌ָ) ___	Kamets ___	a ___	as in Father
◌ֵ ___	Tsiri ___	ai ___	or i long
◌ִי ___	Hhirik long	i ___	as in it
וֹ ___	Cholom ___	oi ___	
וּ ___	Melupum ___	eu ___	as in Mute

2. Five short:

◌ַ ___	Pathach ___	as a in art	
◌ֶ ___	Segol ___	ê ___	
◌ִ ___	Hhiric ___	i ___	short
◌ֻ ___	Kibbuts ___	u ___	must
◌ְ ___	Scheva ___	e or i	short

Cholom is sometimes without ו as לֹא not.
Scheva is pronounced in the beginning of a word as בְּנִי - bini
in the middle of a word after a (:) as תִּלְמְדוּ Tilmedu
is then moveable. In other cases it is quiescent or not sounded.

Mappik,

is a dot in a ה at the end of a word, sign of 3rd pers: sing: fem: poss: pron:
& strengthens the sound.

Dagesh,

is either single or double: the single Dagesh is in the letters בְּגַדְכְּפַת
makes the sound harder: as,

With Dagesh בּ גּ דּ כּ פּ תּ		Double Dagesh may be found in
T. P. K. D. G. B.		any letter except Gutturals & ר
Without Dagesh ב ג ד כ פ ת		and is considered as if written
Th. Ph. Ch. Dh. Gh. V.		twice as לִמֵּד - limmid.

Mak-kaph,

is a small stroke resembling a Hyphen between two words
joining them together, as עַל־פְּנֵי Al-Pini.

Pl. 7.

Arabic:– Vowels and Diacritic Signs.

The Arabic Language has only three Vowels to indicate all vowel sounds..

(´) Fatha ———— sounds as — a . é . or ai

(˛) Casra ———— sounds as — i , ee

(˙) Damma ———— sounds as — o . u . or ou

The Diacritic Signs are;

1. The Jesm — (˛) denotes that the letter over which it is placed has no vowel but is connected with that which precedes it, corresponding to the Hebrew Sheva quiescent, as, فَصْل Faslon.

2. The Teschdid (˛) as the Hebrew Dagesh forte, a sign of doubling the letter — as, تُوَزَّلُ nazzala is written نَزَّلَ

3. The Hamza (ء) The sign of a radical Elif — it always accompanies the vowel which attends ا

4. The Wesla (ٱ) combines the Elif at the beginning of a word with a preceding vowel, — بَيْتُ ٱلْمُقَدَّسِ beito 'lmukeddesi

5. The Medda ٓ implies extension, a sign of lengthening the sound of Elif.

Nunnation or tenwin:

When the Vowels are doubled as (˝) (˷) (˶) they are called Nunnation and are pronounced as, — _an_ , _en_ , _in_ , _on_ or _un_ — but they are only used in the language of the Koran or in the Poetical Style.

Pl. 8

Syriack Vowels.

The Syriack Language has Five Vowels:

			Modern	
ֻ	Petoho	a	÷	÷
ֻ	Rebotso	e	ֻ	ֻ
ֻ	Hebotso	i	ֻ	
ֻ	Skofo	o	ֻ	
ֻ	Etsofo	u	o֊ or o֊	

The two first Vowels may also be placed below the line:

ܸ ha _____ ܷ he _____ ܷ bi _____ ܿ bo _____ ܿ bu _____

All syllables or words are not always accompanied with their vowel figures or points — where they are wanting they must be supplied by

Diphthongs:

ܿ	or ܿ	_____	au
ܿ		_____	eu
ܿ		_____	iu
ܿ		_____	ou
ܿ		_____	ai
ܿ		_____	oi

Linea Occultans,

is a short line placed under letters like the Hebrew pathah (‍) to indicate that the consonant is not to be pronounced — as, ܒܪܬ read Bath not (Barth) Daughter.

Oloph is sounded like Jud when preceded by another Oloph as ܐܐܪ oiar "air". — Jud at the beginning of a word having (‍) is not pronounced as a consonant, but is quiescent as ܝܠܝܦ ileph. he learned not yileph. — Oloph is sometimes prefixed to Jud.

Pl 9

The Article. Hebrew.

The Hebrews have but one Article expressed by הַ with a (־) Pathah prefixed to the noun and a Dagesh in the letter following, as הַשָּׁמַיִם the Heavens.

1. When the letter does not admit of a Dagesh, the article has a Kamets (ָ) as הָאִישׁ the Man.

2. When the article is succeeded by a Kamets, its Pathah is changed into (ֶ) as הֶהָרִים the Mountains.

Gender.

There are two Genders, masculine and feminine. Nouns are sometimes common to both Genders.

· Nouns are Feminine by signification or termination:

1. Names of women . . . . as רָחֵל Rachael
2. . . . . cities . . . . . as צִיּוֹן Tseyoin
3. . . . . countries . . . as כְּנַעַן Kinaan

· Nouns are Masculine, when names of men – offices of men – of Angels – of nations – of rivers – of mountains – of months.

Nouns Common to both Genders are the names of Beasts as בָּקָר Bakar Cattle, צֹאן Sheep – דֹּב a Bear – זְאֵב a Wolf.

Formation of the Feminine.

The feminine is formed by adding ה & a preceding ָ to the masculine, as מַלְכָּה Malcah a Queen, from מֶלֶךְ a King. If the last letter be ה the points only are changed, as יָפֶה : יָפָה fem. When the Masculine ends in י a ת is usually added as מִצְרִי an Egyptian Man מִצְרִית an Egyptian Woman.

Pl.10.

The Article. Arabic.

The Arabians have only one Article and renders the noun to which it is prefixed definite in its sense : ال The

الصخور The Stones

الْمَلِك The King

1. When a noun substantive agrees with an adjective, the article is prefixed likewise to the adjective.

الذهب السبيك The liquid Gold.

2. Proper names do not admit the Article but always accompanies the epithet, should any follow; as, Alexander the Great.

إِبْرَاهِيم الْأَصَّن Abraham the faithful.

3. ل in the article is sometimes dropped, the place being supplied by Teshdid, as

الَّيْل for اللَّيْل The Night.

Gender.

There are only two genders, masculine and feminine. Nouns are feminine by signification or termination.

1. By signification — names of women, as

أُمّ a mother. مَرْيَم Mary.

2. The double members of the Body, as يَد the hand. عَيْن the eye.

3. By termination – 1st in ة as جَنَّة a garden ظُلْمَة darkness.
2d in ا and ي servile حَمْرَآء red أُولَي first.

The Syriack has only one Article, and renders
the noun to which it is prefixed definite in its sense.

ܐ‎ *joth* _ The ⎫ ܐ‎ is often used as emphatic, as
ܣܦܪ‎ *safar, a book.* ܣܦܪܐ‎ *sephro, the book.*

ܡܠܟܐ‎   The King.

Gender.

There are Two genders, the Masculine and Feminine.

Nouns are Feminine which are
1ˢᵗ. The names of women, as   ܚܬܐ‎ *chotho, a sister.*
2.   cities
3.   Nouns of dominion or office, as   ܐܒܗܘܬܐ‎ { *abohutho* _ *paternity.*

Formation of Feminine.

The feminine is formed by adding ܐܬ‎   as
ܐܢܫܐ‎ *nosho* _ *a man;*   ܐܢܬܬܐ‎ *anttho, a woman.*
ܒܪܐ‎ *baro* _ *a son;*   ܒܪܬܐ‎ *bartho, a daughter.*
When this distinction is not observed it is determined by
the context, as   ܐܒܐ‎ *abo* _ *a father;*   ܐܡܐ‎ *emo, a mother.*

Number.

Nouns have two numbers, the Singular and the Plural.
The Plural number in most Nouns is not expressed
by termination. but merely distinguished from the
singular by a diacritical point called Ribbui, as

ܡܠܟܐ‎ *Malchee* _ *Kings.*
ܛܠܝܐ‎ *Teleyee* _ *young children.*
ܢܒܝܐ‎ *Nabihee* _ *Prophets.*
ܟܢܫܐ ܣܓܝܐ‎ *Chenshee sagiee* _ *great multitudes.*

Pl. 12.

Hebrew Nouns.

Nouns are formed in general from the third person singular of the preterite tense of the first conjugation Kal by changing its vowels as דָּבָר a word, from דִּבֶּר he spake. מֶלֶךְ a King, from מָלַךְ he did reign.

Number.

There are Three numbers, Singular, Dual, and Plural.

The Dual is formed by adding to the Singular ־יִם and a Pathah under the preceding letter, as יָד Yad, a hand יָדַיִם Yadayim, two hands.

The Feminine forms its Dual in the same manner — but changes also the ה into ת as שָׂפָה Saphah, a lip — שְׂפָתַיִם Siphathayim, lips.

The Plural of Masculine Nouns is formed by changing the Dual ־יִם into ־יִם. and .־ as מְלָכִים Kings. — דִּבְרֵי אֱלֹהִים Devriy Elohim — the words of God.

The Plural of Feminine Nouns is formed by changing ה into וֹת, as נַעֲרָה a damsel, Plural נַעֲרוֹת damsels.

If the termination be וּת the ו Shurek is changed into a וֹ Cholem with a dageshed י Yod preceding it and a (ֻ) Kibbuts under the preceding letter, as מַלְכִיּוֹת, Plural מַלְכוּת

When two nouns are related to each other so as to require the preposition of between them, the former is governed and undergoes a change, and is said to be in regimen, or contracted.

The Masculine Singular shortens the vowels and the Plural drops the ם as דִּבְרֵי instead of דְּבָרִים

The Feminine Singular changes ה into ת as תּוֹרַת instead of תּוֹרָה The Dual of both genders drops the final ם

Arabic. Nouns.

Formation of Feminine.

Feminines are formed from Masculines by
addition, transposition, or changing of Letters
chiefly by the addition of ة _ رَجُل a man, ة
a woman _ مَالِك a King, مَالِكَة a Queen.
فَتَى fata, a little boy changes ي to ا before ة _ ا
little girl :_ as do many others of this form.

Number.

There are three numbers, Singular, Dual, and
The Dual is formed by adding ان to the Sin
The Plural is either perfect or imperfect.
The perfect is chiefly adopted in proper nam
The regular masculine plural adds ون to
singular, as مُحَمَّد Mohammed مُحَمَّدُون
نَبِي a prophet نَبِيُّون prophets.

The plural of perfect feminines is formed
adding ات as فَرْحَة a cheerful woman ات
cheerful women _ also by changing ة to
ات نَبِيَّات a prophetess نَبِيَّة

The imperfect plurals are such as are not for
by adding ان or ات , and are so irregular
rules can greatly assist the memory.

Case.

1. Fathu doubled ً an _ is the sign of the nominative
2. Casra doubled ٍ in _ . . . . genitive case
3. Damma doubled ٌ an a un _ . . . . . . accusative ca

The Letters so marked are pronounced as if terminated with the let

Hebrew Nouns.

Pl. 14.

Case.

Nouns in Hebrew have no Cases properly so called, made by different terminations as in Greek or Latin; but are varied by particles prefixed as in the following example:— they are the same in the Dual and Plural. שֶׁל is generally used by Rabbinical Writers.

	Singular.	Masc.	בֵּית		Plural.	
			House.			
N.	בֵּית	. . . a House	N.	בָּתִּים	. . .	Houses
G.	שֶׁל-בֵּית	of a . . .	G.	שֶׁל-בָּתִּים	of	
D.	לְבֵּית	. . . to a	D.	לְבָּתִּים	. . . to	
Ac.	אֶת-בֵּית	a . . .	Ac.	אֶת-בָּתִּים		Houses
Voc.	הַבֵּית	o	Voc.	הַבָּתִּים	. . . o	
Abl.	נִבֵּית	from a . . .	Abl.	מִבָּתִּים	. . . from . . .	
	נִן from בְּ in				נִן from בְּ in	

	Singular.	Fem.	מַלְכָּה		Plural.	
			a Queen			
N.	מַלְכָּה	. . . a Queen	N.	מַלְכּוֹת	. . .	Queens
G.	שֶׁל-מַלְכָּה	of a	G.	שֶׁל-מַלְכּוֹת	of	
D.	לְמַלְכָּה	. . . to a . . .	D.	לְמַלְכּוֹת	. . . to	
Ac.	אֶת-מַלְכָּה	the . . .	Ac.	מַלְכּוֹת-אֶת		Queens
Voc.	הַמַלְכָּה	. . . o . . .	Voc.	הַמַלְכּוֹת	. . . o	
Abl.	מִמַלְכָּה	from a . . .	Abl.	נִי מַלְכּוֹת	from	
	בְּ in				נִן from. בְּ in . .	

The לְ , אֶת , מִ and בּ are sometimes used to point out all the Cases except the vocative — and ה is used to point out the genitive and accusative.

Pl.15.

Arabic. Nouns.

Declension.

The declension of Arabic Nouns is exceedingly simple, there being in writing no real difference of case, except in the addition of ا servile to the accusative distinguishing the nominative singular & plural by ٌ , the genitive, dative & ablative by ٍ , and the accusative by ً , the dual ending always in Casra: from these there are a few exceptions.

Singular.	Masc. بَيْتٌ	Plural.
	a House	
N.	بَيْتٌ ... a house	N. بُيُوتٌ ... Houses
G.	بَيْتٍ of a	G. بُيُوتٍ ... of Houses
D.	بَيْتٍ to a	D. بُيُوتٍ to Houses
Acc.	بَيْتًا ... a house	Acc. بُيُوتًا Houses
Abl.	بَيْتٍ from a	Abl. بُيُوتٍ from Houses

The Dual has	بَيْتَانِ	two Houses.

Singular.	Fem. مَلِكَةٌ	Plural.
	a Queen	
N.	مَلِكَةٌ ... a Queen	N. مَلِكَاءُ ... Queens
G.	مَلِكَةٍ of a	G. مَلِكَاتٍ of ....
D.	مَلِكَةٍ to a	D. مَلِكَاتٍ to ....
Acc.	مَلِكَةًا ... a Queen	Acc. مَلِكَاتٍ Queens
Abl.	مِن مَلِكَةٍ from a	Abl. مِن مَلِكَاتٍ from ....

The Genitive, Dative, and Ablative are expressed by the same word, but the two last are for the most part distinguished in construction from the first by certain particles _ a ل &c. for the Dative, and مِن &c. for the Ablative.

The Vocative is expressed by يا prefixed to the Accusative.

Syriack Nouns.

Pl. 16.

Case.

The Cases of Nouns are noted by Prepositions or prefixed letters: the Genitive is mostly expressed by ܕ as ܕܐܪܥܐ dar-ho, of the earth. The Dative by ܠ and is also the sign of the Accusative. The Ablative is expressed by ܡܢ men - from - out of ܒ in, into, with, as ܒܒܝܬܐ bebaitho, in the house: ‿ ܒܥܡܐ ba-mo, among the people.

	Singular. Masc. ܒܝܬܐ		Plural
		a House	
N.	ܒܝܬܐ .... a House	N.	ܒܬܐ .... Houses
G.	ܕܒܝܬܐ ... of a ... or ܕ	G.	ܕܒܬܐ ... of ... or ܕ
D.	ܠܒܝܬܐ to a	D.	ܠܒܬܐ to ....
Acc.	ܠܒܝܬܐ .. a House	Acc.	ܠܒܬܐ ... Houses
Voc	ܐܘ ܒܝܬܐ .... o	Voc.	ܐܘ ܒܬܐ .. o
Abl.	ܡܢ ܒܝܬܐ from a	Abl.	ܡܢ ܒܬܐ from ....

	Singular. Fem. ܡܠܟܬܐ		Plural
		a Queen.	
N.	ܡܠܟܬܐ .. a Queen	N.	ܡܠܟܬܐ .. Queens
G.	ܕܡܠܟܬܐ of a	G.	ܕܡܠܟܬܐ of ....
D.	ܠܡܠܟܬܐ to a	D.	ܠܡܠܟܬܐ to ....
Acc.	ܠܡܠܟܬܐ .. a Queen	Acc.	ܠܡܠܟܬܐ Queens
Voc.	ܐܘ ܡܠܟܬܐ .. o	Voc.	ܐܘ ܡܠܟܬܐ o ....
Abl.	ܡܢ ܡܠܟܬܐ from a	Abl.	ܡܢ ܡܠܟܬܐ from ....

Pl.17.

List of Nouns.

The following words will serve as examples for practice in Declension by using a Card with the usual forms for Number and Case with the spaces cut out the same noun may be declined at the same time in Hebrew, Arabic, and Syriack.

Hebrew	Arabic	Syriack	
דָּבָר	دَبَرْ	؛ܩ؛	a Word
אָב	أُبْ	ܐܰܕܐ abo	a Father
סֵפֶר se-far		ܣܦܰܪ sa-far	a Book
עֶבֶד avad		ܟܰܒܕܐ abdo	a Servant
גֶּבֶר gavar		ܓܰܒܪܐ gabro	a Man
אִשָּׁה esha	Feminine	ܐܰܢܬܬܐ anttho	a Woman
שָׁנָה shana		ܫܰܢܬܐ shantho	a Year
בַּת bath		ܒܰܪܬܐ bartho	a Daughter
אָחוֹת a choith	اِخْتا	ܐܰܚܘܬܐ achotho	a Sister
אֵם	أُمّْ	ܐܶܡܐ	a Mother

The Adjective agrees with its Substantive, in Gender and Number, as

נַעַר טוֹב _a good lad_   נְעָרִים טוֹבִים _good lads_

נַעֲרָה טוֹבָה _a good damsel_   נְעָרוֹת טוֹבוֹת _good damsels_

Degrees of Comparison are Three:
Positive, Comparative, and Superlative.

---

1. Positive, as טוֹב _toiv – good._

---

2. Comparative is formed by prefixing to the noun or adjective belonging to it מִ with a (.) chirik, & a dagesh in the succeeding letter, as

וְהַנָּחָשׁ הָיָה עָרוּם מִכֹּל חַיַּת

And the serpent was more subtle than any beast: –

or by prefixing מִן _Men_ and a maccaph; as

טוֹבִים הַשְּׁנַיִם מִן־הָאֶחָד

Two are better than one.

---

3. The Superlative is formed by joining the word מְאֹד with the adjective, as טוֹב מְאֹד _very good_; Prefixing ב to the noun, as הַטּוֹב בַּנָּשִׁים _Hattoir-Bannashim – The best among Women_; –
Repeating the Adjective; – using two synonymous words; – doubling the noun, as

שְׁמֵי הַשָּׁמַיִם _Shemiy Hashshamayim –_

The heaven of heavens, or the highest heaven.

The Adjective agrees with its Substantive in gender and number.

Degrees of Comparison are Three: Positive, Comparative, and Superlative.

1. Positive, as خير good.

2. Comparative is formed by prefixing ا to the Positive, as اخير better — and takes in general من than after it.

لذنبي اليك عظيم وانت اعظم منه

My offence against thee is great, but thou art greater than it. من does not always immediately follow the Comparative, as اعزّ عندي من بوبوعيني

Dearer to me than the apple of my eye.

Other Particles often follow the Comparative in place of من in feminine of Comp. ي quiescent after Fatha is added in place of ا prefixed, as كُبَرِي greater (fem,) اكبَرُ greater (masc.) كبِير great.

3. The Superlative is formed without من followed by a genitive, as اعدّي the most dangerous. and اذّني

It becomes Superlative where the noun precedes the Adjective, — سعدي اعلم Sadi is most wise or when followed by an article, as احسَنُ النّاس the best of men. اللّهُ اعلمُ God is most wise.

Pl. 20.

1. The Adjective agrees with its Substantive in Gender and Number, as

ܓܒܪܐ ܛܒܐ   Gabro-tobo; a good man.

ܡܠܟܐ ܪܒܐ   Malcho rabo; a great king.

Feminine.

ܐܬܐ ܛܒܬܐ   Atho tobtho; good ground.

ܐܬܐ ܪܒܬܐ   Otho rabtho; a great sign.

Plural Masc.

ܦܐܪܐ ܛܒܐ   Piree tobee; — Good fruits.

ܥܒܕܐ ܫܦܝܪܐ   Ebodee shaphiree — Good works.

Plural. Fem:

ܣܝܡܬܐ ܛܒܬܐ   Simotho tobotho; good treasures.

ܐܬܘܬܐ ܪܘܒܬܐ   Othrotho raubotho; great signs.

2. The Comparative is formed by prefixing the preposi-tions ܐܝܟ aic, as, like ܡܢ men, from, than, more than; as ܐܝܟ ܩܠܐ ܕܡܝܐ .... aic kolo do mayo — as the voice of waters. — ܕܝܬܝܪ ܡܢ ܫܠܝܡܘܢ ܗܪܟܐ darthir men, Sale-mon horco, — a greater than Solomon is here.

3. The Superlative is formed by the Particle ܛܒ tob — very exceedingly — ܛܒ ܡܢ tob men — much more, very much — as ܚܕܘܬܐ ܪܒܬܐ ܕܛܒ hadulho rabtho detob, exceeding great joy.

ܡܠܦܢܐ ܐܝܢܐ ܦܘܩܕܢܐ ܪܒ ܒܢܡܘܣܐ

Malphono, aino pukdono rab benomuso?

Master, which is the great commandment in the law? that is the greatest.

Pl. 21.

Hebrew - Arabic - and Syriack - Pronoun

Hebrew Pronouns are either separable, consisting of distinct words; or inseparable, that is, letters affixed to the noun.

Separable Pronouns are either Personal, Relative, Demonstrative, or Interrogative.

Personal Pronouns, – in which are to be noticed, Gender, Number & Case.

Person	Singular		Person	Plural	
1ˢᵗ	אֲנִי or אָנֹכִי	I Com.	1ˢᵗ	אָנוּ or נַחְנוּ or אֲנַחְנוּ	we C.
2ᵈ	אַתָּה thou M.		2ᵈ	אַתֶּם ye M.	
	אַתְּ thou F.			אַתֵּן ye F. or אַתֵּנָה	
3ʳᵈ	הוּא He M.		3ᵈ	הֵם or הֵמָּה they M.	
	הִיא She F. She			הֵן or הֵנָּה they F.	

Arabic Pronouns are Personal, Relative, and Demonstrative.

The Arabians acknowledge only Three parts of Speech, – including under the Verb; the Noun, the Pronoun, the Participle, and many Adverbs and Prepositions.

Personal Pronouns have the same variation of Gender and Number as Nouns, but have no difference of Case.

Person	Singular		Person	Plural	
1ˢᵗ	أَنَا	... I ... Com.	1ˢᵗ	نَحْنُ	We Com.
2ᵈ	أَنْتَ	... Thou .. M.	2ᵈ	أَنْتُمْ	... You ... M.
	أَنْتِ	... Thou . F.		أَنْتُنَّ	... You .. F.
3ᵈ	هُوَ	.. He	3ᵈ	هُمْ	...They .. M.
	هِيَ	.. She		هُنَّ	...They .. F.

Syriack Pronouns are Personal, Relative, and Demonstrative.

Personal Pronouns have the same variation of Gender and Number as Nouns.

Person	Singular		Person	Plural	
1ˢᵗ	ܐܸܢܵܐ	... I. Com.	1ˢᵗ	ܚܢܲܢ	We Com.
2ᵈ	ܐܲܢ݇ܬ	...Thou M.	2ᵈ	ܐܲܢ݇ܬܘܿܢ	.. Ye M.
	ܐܲܢ݇ܬܝ	.Thou F.		ܐܲܢ݇ܬܹܝܢ	.. Ye F.
3ᵈ	ܗܘܿ	.. He	3ᵈ	ܗܸܢܘܿܢ	...They M.
	ܗܝܼ	... She		ܗܸܢܹܝܢ	...They F.

CPSIA information can be obtained at www.ICGtesting.com
Printed in the USA
LVOW010515201212

312556LV00009B/139/P

9 781290 095709